The Source for Development of Executive Functions

by Gail J. Richard

Skill	Ages	Grades
■ executive functions	■ birth through 18	■ PreK through 12

Evidence-Based Practice

- Executive functions are a group of cognitive skills localized in the frontal lobe structures. Deficits in executive functioning involve both discrete skills and the processes that control the use of these skills (Cicerone et al., 2000).

- Impairments in executive functions may co-occur with a variety of disorders or syndromes including traumatic brain injury (TBI), fetal alcohol, very low birth weight, and attention deficits hyperactivity disorder (ADHD). The speech-language pathologist (SLP) plays a critical role in treating these children as language skills are needed to adapt or compensate for these executive function deficits (Marlowe, 2000).

- Early detection of executive function disorders allows educators and SLPs to implement needed intervention strategies in the preschool years (Isquith, Gioia, & Espy, 2004).

- By the age of four, children with higher language abilities perform better on measures of executive function such as working memory and inhibitory control, thus enabling them to make more advantageous decisions. (Carlson, Davis, and Leach, 2005).

- Children with ADHD present with impairments in executive functions which disrupt working memory, rapid naming, strategy development, and self-correction (Shallice, Marzocchi, Coser, Del Savio, Meuter, & Rumiati, 2002).

- Difficulty with memory, problem solving, and self-monitoring are all deficits commonly seen in the TBI population. Intervention to address these problems can target the underlying cognitive process or may work on compensatory strategies. The SLP must follow a developmental approach to treatment should a TBI occur in childhood or adolescence (Kennedy & Coelho, 2005).

The Source for Development of Executive Functions incorporates these principles and is also based on expert professional practice.

References

Carlson, S.M., Davis, A.C., & Leach, J.G. (2005). Less is more: Executive function and symbolic representation in preschool children. *Psychological Science, 16*(8), 609-616.

Cicerone, K., Dahlberg, C., Kalmar, K., Langenbahn, D., Malec, J., Bergquist, T., et al. (2000). Evidence-based cognitive rehabilitation: Recommendations for clinical practice. *Archives of Physical Medicine & Rehabilitation, 81*(2), 1596-1615.

Isquith, P.K., Gioia, G.A., & Espy, K.A. (2004). Executive function in preschool children: Examination through everyday behavior. *Developmental Neuropsychology, 26*(1), 403-422.

Kennedy, M.R.T., & Coelho, C. (2005). Self-regulation after traumatic brain injury: A framework for intervention of memory and problem solving. *Seminars in Speech and Language, 26*(4), 242-255.

Marlowe, W.B. (2000). An intervention for children with disorders of executive functions. *Developmental Neuropsychology, 18*(3), 445-454.

Shallice, T., Marzocchi, G.M., Coser, S., Del Savio, M., Meuter, R.F., & Rumiati, R.I. (2002). Executive function profile of children with attention deficit hyperactivity disorder. *Developmental Neuropsychology, 21*(1), 43-71.

LinguiSystems

LinguiSystems, Inc.
3100 4th Avenue
East Moline, IL 61244
800-776-4332

FAX: 800-577-4555
Email: service@linguisystems.com
Web: linguisystems.com

Copyright © 2005 LinguiSystems, Inc.

All of our products are copyrighted to protect the fine work of our authors. You may copy the Observational Worksheet as often as needed for your own use with clients. Any other reproduction or distribution of the pages of this book is prohibited, including copying the entire book to use as another primary source or "master" copy.

Printed in the U.S.A.

ISBN 10: 0-7606-0616-1
ISBN 13: 978-0-7606-0616-2

About the Author
Gail J. Richard

Gail J. Richard, Ph.D., CCC-SLP, is a professor and Chair in the Department of Communication Disorders & Sciences at Eastern Illinois University in Charleston, Illinois. Gail's teaching at the university and in workshops around the country focuses on childhood developmental language disorders, especially the autistic spectrum, processing disorders, learning disabilities, medical syndromes, and selective mutism. Prior to 25 years in the university setting, Gail worked in the public schools, serving preschool through high school-aged students. She especially enjoys the diagnostic challenge of differentiating among the various aspects of developmental disorders.

Professional awards include being named as a Fellow of the American Speech-Language-Hearing Association and Illinois Speech-language Hearing Association, Distinguished Alumnus of Southern Illinois University-Carbondale and Eastern Illinois University, and five Faculty Excellence Awards. She has served on the ASHA Legislative Council since 1991; and as an NCAA Faculty Athletics Representative since 1994, currently appointed to the NCAA Division I Management Council.

This is Gail's seventh book in the LinguiSystems' *Source* series. Previous publications with LinguiSystems include *The Source for Autism, The Source for Treatment Methodologies in Autism,* and *The Source for Processing Disorders*. Co-authored publications include *The Source for Syndromes* and *The Source for Syndromes 2* with Deb Reichert-Hoge, *The Source for ADD/ADHD* with Joy Russell, *The Language Processing Test 3* and *Language Processing Kit* with Mary Anne Hanner, and *Differential Assessment of Autism & Other Developmental Disorders (DAADD)* with Lynn Calvert.

Cover Design by Jason Platt • Illustrations by Margaret Warner • Page Layout Design by Lisa Parker • Edited by Barb Truman

About the Author
Jill K. Fahy

Jill Fahy, M.A., CCC-SLP, recently joined the faculty at Eastern Illinois University in Charleston, Illinois. After an undergraduate degree in foreign languages, she discovered the field of speech-language pathology and completed her master's degree at the University of Illinois. Jill's previous clinical experience includes work in medical settings in Illinois and Virginia, as well as affiliation with several academic programs as a clinical supervisor and adjunct faculty member.

Jill's clinical background focused primarily on the treatment of communicative, social, and vocational impairments associated with acquired brain injuries. At Eastern, Jill teaches graduate courses in developmental executive functions, motor speech disorders, and clinical methods. Her clinical caseload includes overseeing therapy services for a wide range of children and adolescents with deficits in executive functions, all of whom are working to develop adaptive life skills for the future.

This is Jill's first publication with LinguiSystems and her first collaboration with Gail.

Acknowledgments

We would like to express appreciation to our graduate assistants, Candice Bilson, Manda Geerts, and Brittany Cave for their assistance in keeping Jill's office somewhat organized during this process and for tracking down multiple references. We would also like to thank several student clinicians, Kate Bachhuber, Michelle Beglin, Caroline Dahlstrom, Erin Gaughan, Manda Geerts, Shelly Ginder, Angie Peters, Michelle Repking, and Rudyard Watson, for gracefully meeting the challenges to provide therapy services to the children who served as case studies in this text. We also gratefully acknowledge the tireless efforts of the families of these children and thank them for the opportunity to watch their children grow and develop. Jill would like to particularly thank her mother Linda, daughter Kate, and Mark for their support, time, and understanding.

Table of Contents

Preface 5

Introduction 7

Chapter 1—Defining Executive Functions 13
    Operational Definitions 13
    Components of Executive Functions 14
    Problems in Executive Functions 17
    Anatomy of Executive Functions 20
    Physiology of Executive Functions 24

Chapter 2—Development of Executive Functions 32
    Frontal Lobe Development 34
    Executive Function Development 36
    Cognitive Development 43
    Development of Self-Control 47

Chapter 3—Co-Morbidity of Executive Functions with Other Disorders 49
    Autism and Executive Functions 52
    Asperger's Syndrome/Nonverbal Learning Disorder and Executive Functions 53
    Attention Deficit/Hyperactivity Disorder (ADD/ADHD) and Executive Functions 55
    Fetal Alcohol Syndrome (FAS) and Executive Functions 57
    Tourette's Syndrome and Executive Functions 58
    Williams Syndrome and Executive Functions 60
    Fragile X Syndrome and Executive Functions 61
    Childhood Traumatic Brain Injury and Executive Functions 63

Chapter 4—Assessment of Executive Functions 66
    Executive Function Assessment Principles 66
        Deficits in fundamental language skills 66
        Strengths and weaknesses 67
        Specific executive function skills 67
        Developmental expectations 68
        Impact of intelligence level 69
        Process versus product 70
    Review of Assessment Instruments 70

Table of Contents

    Informal Assessment of Executive Functions 77
        Interviews and Conversations 78
            Sample Interview Questions for Parent or Caregiver 80
            Sample Interview Questions for Teacher 82
            Sample Interview Questions for Child 83
        Observation of Problem Solving Skills 84
        Observation of Social Interaction 92
        Executive Function Skills Evaluation Worksheet 95
    Assessment Case Examples 100

Chapter 5—Global Treatment Approach 118
    Educating Caregivers and Teachers 120
    Environmental Modifications 121
    Increasing Self-Awareness and Self-Regulation 123
    Compensatory Techniques and Strategies 126
    Specific Language / Communication Objectives 128
    Lowering / Modifying Expectations 130
    Teaching the Specific Executive Function Skills 133
    Blending the Treatment Options into a Cohesive Plan 135

Chapter 6—Functional Strategies and Goals 136
    Attention Deficits 139
    Impulsivity/Impaired Inhibition 145
    Impaired Self-Awareness & Self-Monitoring 150
    Deficits in Flexibility 155
    Deficits in Goal Selection 159
    Impaired Initiation 161
    Deficits in Perception and Expression of Social and Environmental Cues 165
    Case Study Treatment Plans 169

Summary 179

Resources for Formal and Informal Assessment 185

References 187

Preface

In recent years, there has been an explosion of literature, articles, recommendations, and diagnostic labels being generated using the term **executive functions**. Historically, the assessment and treatment of executive functions focused on adults who were being treated in response to some type of acquired brain injury to the frontal lobes. As the prevalence of treatment goals targeting executive functions in acquired deficits increased, awareness regarding this category of skills also grew.

Over time, professionals began to acknowledge the same types of deficits being evidenced in children with developmental delays. Children with a variety of developmental disorders were exhibiting a pattern of behaviors identified as deficits in executive functions. The primary difference was that in children, the skills categorized as executive functions were not being acquired; in adults, the deficit referred to a loss of skills as a result of acquired injury.

Educational and medical professionals are increasingly labeling children with clusters of adaptive and self-regulatory behavioral deficits as having impairments in executive functions. As parents seek answers, clinicians and educators must be able to address a variety of questions. What are executive functions? How do I treat deficits in this area? What are the functional implications and desired outcomes I can hope to achieve?

Disruption in the executive functions can, at the very least, limit generalization of therapy skills to the rest of the world. Executive functions actually encompass a large number of communication and social skills, which are critical components of academic and life-adaptive success of executive functions. These skills ultimately allow the child to integrate discrete abilities into a functional whole.

This book seeks to provide a context for understanding executive functions—how they present, how to assess them, and how to treat them in children with a wide array of developmental communication disorders.

Introduction

Executive functions are dynamic, interactive, evolving skills in an individual. When they work well, the result is goal-directed behavior that is appropriate to a given situation and circumstance. Performance is constantly appraised and altered to reflect varying degrees of success or failure, and to respond to unexpected changes in the situation. Executive functions collectively result in the ability to inhibit poorly planned or impulsive behaviors and to sustain successful, goal-oriented behaviors in the context of the everyday environment.

The prefrontal section of the frontal lobe guides us through our day. It can behave with purposeful intent or it can run wild. Three different analogies to clarify the role of executive functions follow.

Driving Analogy

Imagine yourself on the freeway, perhaps on your daily commute or on a trip. You have a destination; you have established a plan to get to your destination; and you are able to safely navigate among unexpected detours or errant drivers. You are aware of the need to accelerate or slow down and can time these actions to avoid disastrous consequences. The journey demands a constant balancing act between incoming sensory information about the environment around you, your own internal urges or frustrations, the success or failure of your driving skills, and the frequent changes in direction required by road signs along the way. When all these variables are juggled appropriately, the result is a fluid, dynamic road trip that allows you to arrive safely at your destination.

Now consider an alternative to the above scenario. This time you are driving without direction; you have no plan. In fact, you may not even recall where it is you are supposed to be going or when you're expected to arrive. You drive aimlessly, missing important road signs, taking wrong turns, and bolting through tollbooths. You alarm other drivers as you drift in and out of lanes, erratically speeding up or slowing down. Perhaps you come to a complete halt, stuck in the freeway of life as you sit in the middle lane, unable to proceed. Maybe you are running on high-octane fuel, speeding so fast you cannot possibly process all the incoming information. Your actual driving ability might be completely functional, but the ability to make appropriate plans to effectively execute the trip is impaired. To make matters worse, you have limited awareness of your situation and proceed under the misguided impression that all is well, even when you succumb to impulsive road rage behavior.

The Source for Development of Executive Functions
Copyright © 2005 LinguiSystems, Inc.

Introduction

Now consider some of the children on your caseload. How many of them are driving through each day without a plan? They are spinning their wheels in vain attempts to execute simple tasks in the classroom, at home, or in other social situations without awareness of how futile their efforts are. The result is poor performance and frustration despite going through the appropriate motions. The isolated discrete skills are intact (i.e., driving ability) but the functional outcome is a complete failure and waste of time and energy.

Orchestra Analogy

Consider another analogy for executive functions—an orchestra. With an optimal blend of talented, well-trained musicians and a dynamic, attentive, multi-tasking conductor, the result can be sublime. Each instrumental section is composed of musicians who have mastered the art of playing their instruments and reading complex musical notation. The discrete skill of producing harmonious notes from the musical instrument has been acquired as a prerequisite to being a member of the orchestra. Reading a musical score is another discrete skill that each musician must have acquired to a certain level of competence to qualify for inclusion in the orchestra. As a member of an orchestra, a musician must integrate a series of discrete isolated skills into a functional whole. Competent musicians in an orchestra are skilled at listening to others around them, taking direction from the conductor, and merging technical requirements with artistic expression.

The conductor must simultaneously divide his attention among the many instruments and parts to perform the near-magic of organizing possible chaos into aesthetic beauty. The task is demanding, necessitating a sustained focus with attention to detail. Each performance requires the conductor to constantly monitor and revise the timing and blending of each individual musician's and section's contribution. A conductor is skilled at processing multiple channels of incoming information. He must integrate previous experience with each new piece the orchestra attempts so that he can identify and rectify any gaps or problems. The conductor needs to recognize strengths and weaknesses within the orchestra as a whole and compensate to achieve a satisfactory result.

Well-trained musicians, led by a highly skilled conductor, can build a repertoire of musical styles and complexities. An orchestra can become very adept at performing certain types or genres of music. Additionally, they can improvise, creating new variations on a theme when necessary. Performances can be impromptu or planned, but the result is fluid and coordinated. For the audience, the cumulative experience is satisfying and harmonious.

Introduction

In the event that some musicians in the orchestra are unprepared for the demands required to achieve a well-integrated performance, the result is likely to be less successful. Imagine the sound of poorly-played violas, cellos, flutes, violins, tympanis, French horns, trombones, and trumpets sounding off simultaneously in different keys and rhythms. No matter how gifted the conductor might be, the end result will not meet the anticipated expectations. Despite some skilled performances, the functional outcome will be in deficit.

A similar scenario could result if the conductor, rather than the musicians, is lacking in skill. Without the leadership of a competent orchestra conductor, the coordination and awareness of timing, balance, and integration of parts to achieve a satisfying whole are absent. If the orchestra is lacking order and organized direction, each section can freely play whatever they choose. The woodwinds might be engaged in the mellow smoothness of a laid-back jazz piece, while the strings are competing for the audience with a fiercely fast rendition of a classical overture. The percussion section doesn't know who to follow. The horn section is also confused and not sure whether to play, be silent, wait, or simply leave. To further add to the chaos, the conductor continues waving his baton, oblivious to the surrounding confusion. If the conductor persists with the same ineffective attempts to coordinate and integrate the various instrumental sections, frustration and behavior problems are likely to erupt.

It is important for the conductor to pay attention to feedback from the audience and musicians in the orchestra and learn from his mistakes. Preparing the orchestra for its next performance requires a careful analysis of exactly where and why the breakdown occurred. Do the musicians need work on their discrete primary skills? Are the prerequisites to a successful performance in place? Does the conductor require help in discriminating the productive versus nonproductive aspects of the orchestra's performance? Perhaps someone should provide an objective opinion or critique to point out to the conductor what is obvious to the audience. Some assistance is required to effectively organize the primary ability of the musicians with the integration capacity of the conductor. The deficit lies in the ability to organize the multiple talents available into a single, eloquent, focused entity that moves smoothly from one musical action to the next.

Language Analogy

A child may acquire normal language skills and, like the orchestra member, be able to demonstrate skill on specific discrete isolated tasks. Establishing a language foundation is prerequisite to engaging in successful, appropriate communicative experiences. Yet,

Introduction

the specific isolated skills might not translate into language competence in a connected environmental situation. Being able to generate antonyms in an isolated language subtest is very different from being able to discern the subtle aspects of connected discourse. Communication demands a grasp of the subtle, unspoken message. That message can change, depending on circumstance and context. Competent language skills also demand flexibility, on-the-spot restructuring, and formatting-to-go. Children who have mastered phonetics, syntax, and semantics in context-free environments may not be able to competently blend into the orchestra of communication demands in real life.

The communication profile associated with Asperger's syndrome provides an illustrative example of a deficit in executive function. Individuals with Asperger's syndrome demonstrate normal skills in fundamental language aspects, with the exception of pragmatics. Measurements suggest competency in basic syntax, semantics, phonology, and morphology. Standard scores tend to be age commensurate or advanced of chronological age expectations. However, the practical management of using those language skills in a functional context is problematic. Language fundamentals are applied in a rigid, inflexible manner.

In the "Asperger" orchestra, the musicians are capable of playing a given repertoire of notes, but the conductor is unable to reorganize the musical talents into other pieces or integrate them into a pleasing variation on the usual presentation style for that musical selection. The piece must always be presented in the exact, same manner. An audience listening to this concert finds itself on the receiving end of a repetitive soliloquy, just as the communication partners of children with Asperger's syndrome do. The higher order integration of language skills with contextual demands and self-awareness is missing.

Now consider a child who presents with deficits in both language and executive functions. In other words, the child has impairments in the structural components of language in addition to disorganization in the ability to integrate and apply language skills. The dual deficits compound the challenges for this student.

Children with Williams syndrome typically exhibit expressive language that is superior to receptive language. Following a delayed onset of language development, their course of language acquisition reflects a splintered pattern of impressive vocabulary and syntax, combined with deficits in semantics and overall comprehension. They evidence a command of expressive language that is fluent, highly embellished, and produced with flair but lacks the comprehension and subtlety necessary for effective communication.

Introduction

To further confuse matters, the overall cognitive profile for children with Williams syndrome is similarly splintered. Their outgoing, gregarious social skills often mask underlying difficulty with basic concepts and big-picture reasoning. Their impulsive problem-solving skills reflect limited planning and organization. In this orchestra, performances are theatric, exciting, and fast-paced. Musicians are likely to perform eloquent and inspiring renditions that are completely independent of their fellow orchestra members. These performers lack the capacity to listen to one another and fail to recognize cues or direction from the conductor, who is experiencing his own difficulties in maintaining order. This audience is in for an impressive but ultimately disorganized and incomplete performance that fails to satisfy. In this case, a lack of full-scale comprehension of meaning in language, coupled with disorganized management and integration, results in ineffective functional communication, despite good expressive production skills.

Identifying the point at which effective communication breaks down is vital to planning effective treatment. The development of language is fostered and shaped every day in every interaction. Real life introduces language in a natural context, where meaning can be derived and conveyed from the unique circumstances of the situation. The natural outcome of effective communication determines a child's ability to function successfully in the world.

To optimize the effects of treatment, differential evaluation of the primary communication deficit is essential. Is the child lacking the isolated discrete language foundation skills of semantics, syntax, phonology, morphology, and/or pragmatics? Is it the nonverbal, inferred processing skills that are lacking? Is the deficit in the application of integration, executive function, and self-regulation of these language fundamentals? Or is it a combination of these variables that are causing the problems?

Optimal treatment cannot be designed until differential analysis of language skills is completed. Effective functional communication must blend mastery of language fundamentals with executive functions to facilitate academic and social success. Children must have the tools to adequately generate, refine, and comprehend basic language fundamentals (semantics, syntax, phonology, morphology, and pragmatics). This is analogous to providing individual music lessons to master production of notes on a musical instrument. Then the child has to proceed to a higher level of performance expectations.

Introduction

Now the child must function as a conductor with an ability to read the audience and elicit the best from each individual musician. In language, a child must be able to read a communicative situation, modify input based on reactions, and effectively manage and coordinate each individual aspect of language. If the child is able to integrate and coordinate all her language skills, the result can be a satisfying and fulfilling interaction. If the child fails to effectively integrate all the language variables, embarrassment and frustration are likely to result.

Children with language deficits often need to be taught how to successfully integrate language skills in unique environments and contexts. This is the role of executive function for the speech-language pathologist—to develop the ability to successfully monitor, manage, and integrate language in relation to behavior. This important step is often overlooked in treatment plans. Discrete specific skills are taught, children demonstrate competence on isolated subtests during evaluation procedures, and they are dismissed from services. However, a teacher continues to experience difficulty, and the therapy progress demonstrated on discrete language skills doesn't generalize to result in positive changes in an academic environment. Parents continue to observe difficulty in social situations for the same reason.

Language therapy must extend beyond remediation of specific isolated skills and must insure the integration and coordinated management offered by executive functions to blend discrete abilities into functional life situations. Only then will the language orchestra achieve its full potential and produce a satisfying, cathartic performance.

Gail and Jill

Chapter 1
Defining Executive Functions

Operational Definitions

In the last ten years, an explosion of research in the normal and disordered development of frontal lobe functions in children has yielded a wealth of information linking deficits in executive functions with a variety of disabilities. Examples of diagnoses that include deficits in executive functions as a component of the disorder include autism, Asperger's, attention deficit disorders, conduct disorder, Tourette's, fetal alcohol syndrome, and childhood schizophrenia, just to name a few.

Once you have a functional understanding of exactly what executive functions are, it becomes easier to recognize deficits in executive functions when they occur in individuals. The acquired version of executive function disorder in adults mirrors what is observed in children with developmental disorders that have an executive function component.

> An operational definition would be that executive functions are a cluster of cognitive skills rooted in the prefrontal structures of the frontal lobe. They include the ability to anticipate consequences, generate novel solutions, initiate appropriate actions or responses to situations, monitor the ongoing success or failure of one's behavior, and modify performance based on unexpected changes. Executive functions are reflected in such processes as developing plans for future actions, retaining these plans and action sequences in working memory until they are executed, and inhibiting irrelevant actions (Pennington & Ozonoff 1996).

Additionally, executive functions integrate relevant prior learning with current motivational or affective states and external conditions. They then modulate an appropriate response or behavior to these conditions. The entire process orchestrated by executive functions is fluid and dynamic, enabling a person to reflect on his actions and to execute some form of organized control over them.

The prefrontal cortex represents the area of the brain responsible for decision making and implementation of strategies. All processed information is channeled into the frontal lobe for integration, assessment of priority, weighting of outcomes, and, eventually, organization of efforts. The end result must be structured to meet some predetermined external criteria or goal.

Defining Executive Functions

Goals can be simple or complex, routine or novel. They are usually driven by social, academic, vocational, or personal points of reference. For example, a child must learn to refrain from hitting a teacher when angry, to complete homework assignments, to do household chores, or to participate in society within cultural and moral rules.

Because goals and surrounding circumstances change over time, the demand on executive functions to achieve a desired outcome will vary. As a task becomes more routine, it requires less self-regulation from executive functions to be successful. Tasks that are novel, more complicated, or accompanied by more distraction will require a greater degree of executive control in order to meet the desired outcomes.

Defining executive functions is generally accomplished by listing components associated with it, although such a list can vary depending on the construct used to organize the components. Some models list broad cognitive processes, such as attention and working memory, alongside those of the executive functions system, ranking them as equal in the outline of regulatory behaviors that govern action. Other definitions list these cognitive processes separately, reflecting the theory that attention and working memory serve as a foundation upon which specific executive functions are acquired. In this case, the cognitive processes of attention and working memory are distinguished from specific executive functions, such as planning and organizing, generating solutions, and developing strategies.

No matter how you divide it up, the overall purpose of our executive functions is to drive goal-oriented and appropriate behaviors within a given time and circumstance. An operational definition of executive functions and the delineation of these components is necessary in order to identify potential areas for assessment and treatment goals. In particular, the generalization of outcomes often depends upon identifying exactly which executive function skill has yet to mature (e.g., self-awareness).

Components of Executive Functions

Attention, inhibition, and working memory are cognitive processes associated with and key to the effective development and use of executive functions. Table 1.1 (page 15) presents a list of those skills involved in executive functions. It includes both the underlying cognitive processes and specific components of executive functions.

Defining Executive Functions

Table 1.1 Executive Functions

Cognitive Processes

Attention	• Focuses, directs, sustains, and selectively attends to relevant stimuli • Shifts attentional focus as required
Inhibition	• Prevents impulsive responses and behaviors • Inhibits disruptive, unwanted, unintentional, irrelevant actions • Delays desirable behaviors until required
Working Memory	• Holds and processes information long enough to execute desired behavior

Components

Goal Selection	• Anticipates consequences and predicts outcomes • Chooses goal based on priority, relevance, experience, and knowledge of current expectation and limitations
Planning & Organizing	• Generates steps, sequences, materials required, and necessary information to execute task or behavior • Creates relevant strategies to meet goal
Initiation & Persistence	• Initiates and maintains goal-directed behavior despite intrusions, distractions, or changes in task demands
Flexibility	• Demonstrates adaptability in strategic thinking and problem solving as goal or environment change • Shifts attention and plans accordingly
Execution & Goal Attainment	• Successfully executes plan and strategies (original and revised) within constraints of environment or time
Self-Regulation	• Applies self-observation to monitor performance, self-judgment to evaluate performance, and self-reaction to change in order to achieve ultimate goal

The Source for Development of Executive Functions
Copyright © 2005 LinguiSystems, Inc.

Defining Executive Functions

Charts and lists tend to divide these components into separate pieces, giving the impression that executive skills are entirely individual and work in a linear fashion. However, in reality, these components are not so easily separated. In addition, they don't occur in a specific linear time frame during the course of solving a problem or determining an appropriate behavior. Executive functions are adaptable, flexible, and work simultaneously in layers over one another to meet the demands of the environment. Cognitive processes, such as attention and inhibition, are constantly being utilized to offer the underlying support necessary for the prefrontal cortex to do its job. Working memory must be engaged throughout the task execution, as the student uses self-talk to hold plans in mind long enough to successfully initiate and finish the response.

In addition to being dependent on and interactive with attention, inhibition, and working memory, most executive function strategies are mediated through verbal language. Self-talk is often used to support a student's efforts in developing strategies, solutions, and monitoring actions. A student needs to internally generate reminders and direct behavior throughout the school day, and then again once he is at home or elsewhere after school. For example, the student must tell himself to pay attention to the teacher, prepare for a test, get his homework done, and plan for an upcoming project. At home, a child must follow the expected order and rules of the household. As a child gets older, he needs to learn how to meet and interact with peers and adults on a regular basis and to meet higher expectations. As tasks become more complex and expectations of performance increase, the ability to use language as a self-guiding system becomes even more critical. The role of language is critical in mediating executive functions and cognitive processes in order to maximize outcome.

The common components of executive functions that are generally agreed upon by various authors include the following:

- Recognizing the need to take some form of action
- Initiating relevant actions while inhibiting destructive actions
- Monitoring and modulating behavior to meet changes in circumstances

The "short version" for defining executive functions has also been offered by various authors. Some examples follow:

- "enable the generation of appropriate behaviors under novel circumstances in a developmental progression" (Marlowe 2000)

Defining Executive Functions

- "formulation of intention and the orchestration of behaviors necessary to attain goals" (Luria 1973)

- "final end point for visual, auditory, somesthetic sensory systems" (Nauta 1971)

- "a number of processes, including organization, planning, monitoring, and execution of purposeful, goal-directed activities" (Lezak 1983)

- "the learning of how" (Stuss 1992)

- "cognition is the 'what' of information; executive functions are the 'where, why, when, and how' of information" (Eslinger 1996)

It should be apparent that **executive functions** is an umbrella term for a collective group of abilities that we use to establish new patterns of behavior to function successfully within the social boundaries of a culture. As circumstances become more familiar, the once-effortful planning and monitoring required to interact appropriately becomes a routine schema, called up to assist us in carrying out the task required. With novel, unexpected, or more complex tasks, executive functions become the key to whether or not we navigate circumstances and situations successfully.

Problems in Executive Functions

All aspects of executive functions are important in the development of a child's ability to demonstrate appropriate judgment, behavior, and decision making. This includes his ability to engage in creative learning and problem solving; to manage behavior at home, school, and in the community; to maintain safety and success by inhibiting impulsive actions and anticipating consequences; and to understand important social cues from the external environment. Children, both typical and atypical, use strategies and self-regulation to ensure success in these environments in order to achieve their life potential.

Our behavior is mediated at the highest level of integration—metacognition—which relies on developmentally intact cognitive and linguistic functions. Children must be able to reflect upon themselves and the environment at a higher level of complexity and independence as they grow older. Assessment requires careful analysis of which components of executive functions are deficit; intervention requires the use of language-specific goals that promote a more complex level of self-awareness and regulation.

The Source for Development of Executive Functions

Defining Executive Functions

Successfully treating deficit executive functions and promoting functional improvements require the ability to analyze whether a child has impairments in executive functions, cognitive processes, linguistic functions, or a combination of all three. Children with executive function deficits often show poor awareness of their strengths or weaknesses. They may have difficulty recognizing or determining relevant and advantageous goals for themselves, or may be unable to identify consequences of their behaviors. Beyond that, they may understand the negative outcomes of their performance, but be unable to initiate, plan, organize, or execute more effective actions. Some children will "shut down" physically and verbally, literally unable to find a way to initiate whatever plan they may have been able to generate. Inattention, distractibility, or impulsivity may contribute to identifying only part of an assignment. Poor self-monitoring may contribute to problems as well; if a child is unable to recognize that his efforts are ineffective, he may persist with strategies or plans that no longer meet the ultimate goal of a situation. Consider that language deficits might also be present, compounding the problem. The child may be limited by an inability to comprehend tasks at the level of complexity required, or may be unable to self-cue because of his limited expressive language capabilities.

In general, children with impairments in executive functions often experience a wide array of breakdowns, which ultimately limit the degree of achievement and independence they attain in life. Their potential for meeting educational, vocational, and community expectations often relies on how aware they are of deficits, how well they use strategies to compensate, and how consistently they regulate their actions. Table 1.2 (page 19) illustrates functional skills that may be impaired or limited by deficits in executive function capacity.

These limitations may be seen in school, at home, and in the community. Children who experience pragmatic, communicative, reasoning, memory, and learning deficits—due to disorders with specific or indirect limitations in executive functions—often find themselves unable to effectively control or improve their performance. They may find it difficult to follow rules and expectations, leading to problems with discipline and transition. Social encounters may require excessive direction and modeling from parents. As a child grows, his ability to learn self-care tasks or to solve more complex problems may be delayed or fail to develop, leading to compromised independence. Deficits in the ability to self-regulate and self-monitor will automatically mean the child needs more supervision than others. Put all of this together and you have a recipe for failure in academics and, ultimately, community participation and vocational self-sufficiency.

Table 1.2 Impairments Associated With Deficits in Executive Functions

Communication

- Disorganized discourse (either verbose or incomplete)
- Tangential, wandering narratives lacking in point and sequence
- Failure to comprehend main theme or idea despite understanding specific words or sentences
- Reduced ability to use self-talk as means of verbally mediating cognition and executive functions
- Inattentive, impulsive listening affects comprehension or memory
- Lack of initiation limits completeness of communication

Pragmatics & Social Interaction

- Poor ability to take others' perspective
- Inability to transition
- Impaired recognition of nonverbal or subtle cues
- Poor inhibition of impulsive desires or plans
- Inaccurate judgment of situations
- Inappropriate, impulsive, or dangerous behavior

Processing & Reasoning

- Limited abstract reasoning
- Difficulty recognizing relevant vs. irrelevant input
- Difficulty drawing conclusions and making inferences
- Limited divergent thinking
- Limited ability to predict consequences or outcomes

Problem Solving & Learning

- Impaired strategic thinking
- Limited ability to generate multiple solutions
- Difficulty generalizing to other contexts
- Trouble learning from consequences
- Impaired ability to carry out instructions or tasks to completion
- Impulsive attempts with failed outcomes
- Unable to recognize failure or the need to revise strategies

Memory

- Difficulty retaining information long enough to execute steps
- Forget to execute tasks or be where necessary at a given time
- Recall information out of sequential or temporal order, including verbal directions
- Failure to integrate long-term memories of past experiences into future decisions

Defining Executive Functions

How well a child performs in any given situation is determined by an audience of "judges." Evaluation is informally conducted by teachers, parents, peers, and other people present in a situation. The challenge for a professional is to attempt to identify the source of the behavior breakdown. The deficit could be at the level of basic language development; it could be in general cognition; it could be in processing aspects of a situation; it could be at a level of integrating all the environmental and internal stimuli present; or it could be in the ultimate mediation and regulation of resultant behaviors.

One of the key steps in identifying executive function deficits in children is to better understand the specific brain structures involved in the normal acquisition and development of these skills. The next section discusses the anatomical and physiological components involved in executive functions.

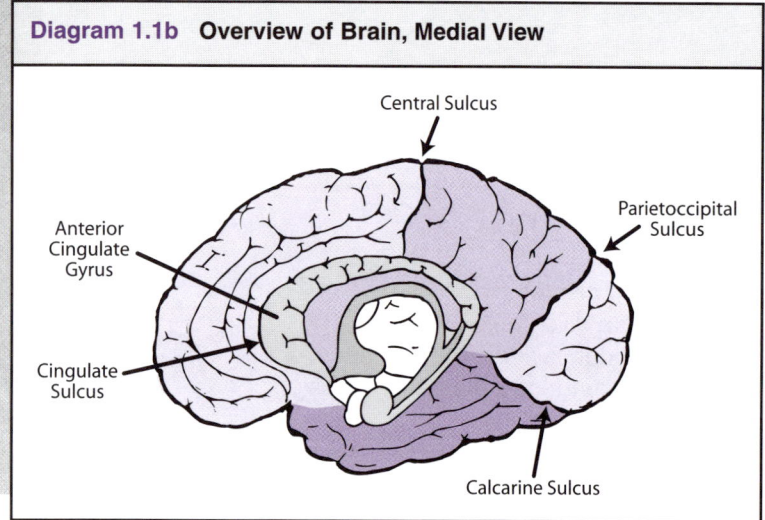

Diagram 1.1a Overview of Brain, Lateral View

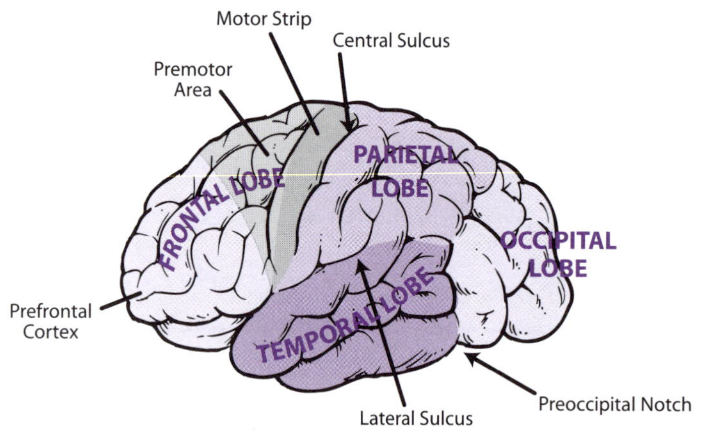

Diagram 1.1b Overview of Brain, Medial View

Anatomy of Executive Functions

The source of executive functioning lies in the prefrontal cortex, which is part of the frontal lobe, and its connections to other parts of the brain. The frontal lobe is the most recently evolved part of the human brain. It is singularly larger in the human species than in other primates, making up nearly half of the cerebral cortex. The frontal lobe controls what we do with our bodies physically through muscular movements, and socially through behavioral responses.

Most of us have studied and are familiar with the motor and premotor sections of the frontal lobe, which are responsible for selecting, directing, and generating movement. (Diagrams 1.1a and 1.1b)

The Source for Development of Executive Functions
Copyright © 2005 LinguiSystems, Inc.

Defining Executive Functions

The prefrontal cortex is the anterior-most part of the frontal lobe, found just anterior to the premotor strip, and comprises much of the frontal lobe itself. It is the prefrontal cortex of the frontal lobe that mediates temporal organization of selected behaviors within a given situation or context-dependent behavior. The prefrontal cortex is responsible for premotor cognitive decisions and for integrating relevant prior learning and motivational states with incoming information about the environment. The prefrontal cortex is the part of the brain that allows children to consciously self-regulate and modify impulses to fit the requirements of society.

How does it do this? The frontal lobe, specifically the prefrontal cortex, is the final end point for most incoming information, as well as internal states of being. The prefrontal cortex shares an extensive network of connections with other cortical and subcortical areas. Anatomical links exist between the prefrontal cortex and association areas in the temporal, parietal, and occipital lobes. Connections also exist between the prefrontal cortex and other parts of the frontal lobe, as well as subcortical structures including the limbic system, the thalamus, the hippocampus, amygdala, and hypothalamus. These connections are both afferent and efferent, meaning that the connections receive information from other parts of the brain and then send directional messages back to those same structures. As such, the prefrontal cortex can influence messages within the brain that result in behavioral changes within a social situation.

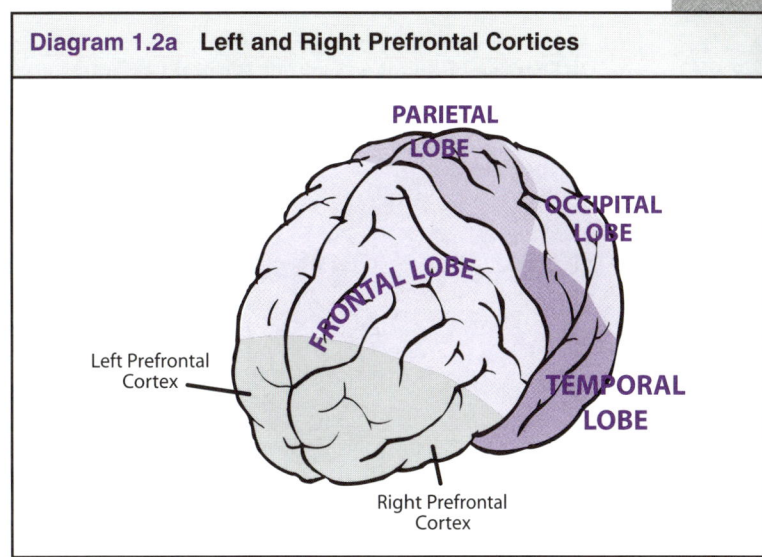

Diagram 1.2a   Left and Right Prefrontal Cortices

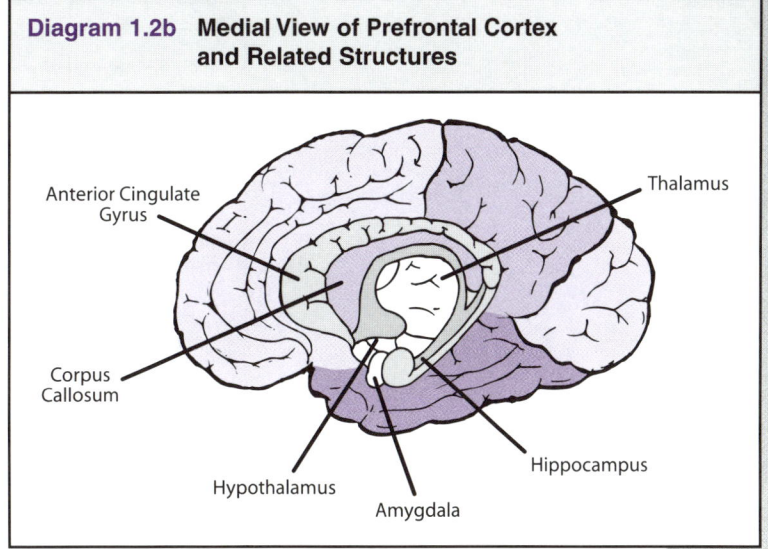

Diagram 1.2b   Medial View of Prefrontal Cortex and Related Structures

The Source for Development of Executive Functions
Copyright © 2005 LinguiSystems, Inc.

Defining Executive Functions

The frontal lobe is often defined and divided by its anatomy. Those sections, moving anteriorly from the central sulcus, include the primary motor cortex (area 4), the premotor cortex (the lateral surface of area 6), the supplementary motor cortex (the medial surface of area 6), the frontal eye fields (area 8), the motor speech (Broca's) cortex (area 44), and the prefrontal cortex. The prefrontal cortex lies anterior to the premotor cortex. It includes Brodmann's areas 9, 10, 11, 12, 24, 25, 32, 44, 45, 46, and 47. Diagrams 1.3a and 1.3b illustrate the major components of the frontal lobe.

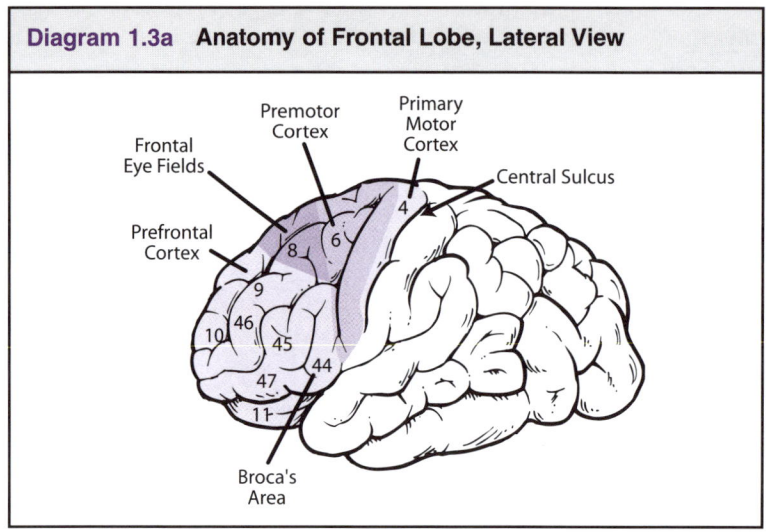

Diagram 1.3a Anatomy of Frontal Lobe, Lateral View

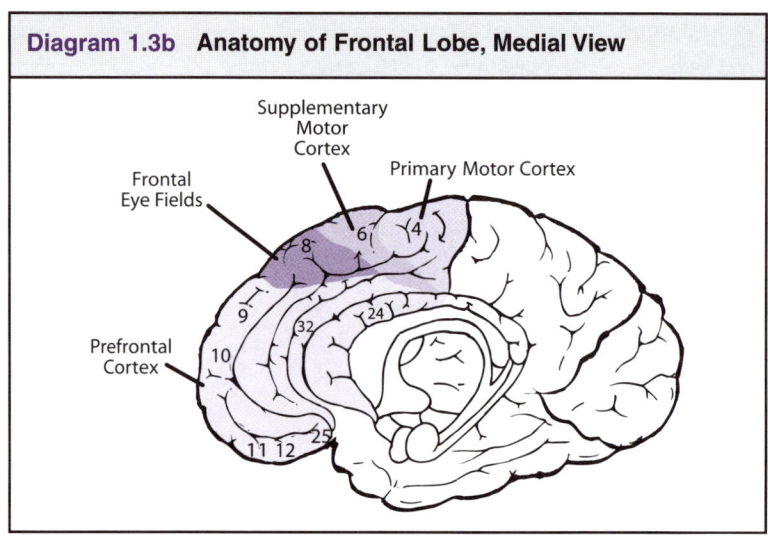

Diagram 1.3b Anatomy of Frontal Lobe, Medial View

Defining Executive Functions

The prefrontal cortex itself is further divided into sections, each of which links to and modulates different higher order processes of cognition and executive functioning. These areas occupy, in general, the anterior-most part of the frontal lobe, wrap around the lateral portion, and go deep to the lower and medial surfaces of the frontal lobe. In general, there are two major functional divisions of the prefrontal cortex: **orbitofrontal cortex** and **dorsolateral cortex**. It should be noted that these divisions can be further segmented and do not necessarily reflect black and white delineations of anatomy. They are, rather, generally agreed upon areas that reflect an ever-growing body of research into the functional physiology of each part of the prefrontal cortex. Diagrams 1.4a and 1.4b illustrate the orbitofrontal and dorsolateral prefrontal cortex areas.

The orbitofrontal cortex encompasses Brodmann's areas 11, 12, 24, 25, 32, and 47 and occupies the anterior medial and ventral parts of the prefrontal cortex. It is sometimes divided into the medial frontal section (areas 25 and 32), or the ventromedial section (areas 11, 12, 13, 25, and 32), or the paralimbic cortex (areas 12, 24, 25, and 32).

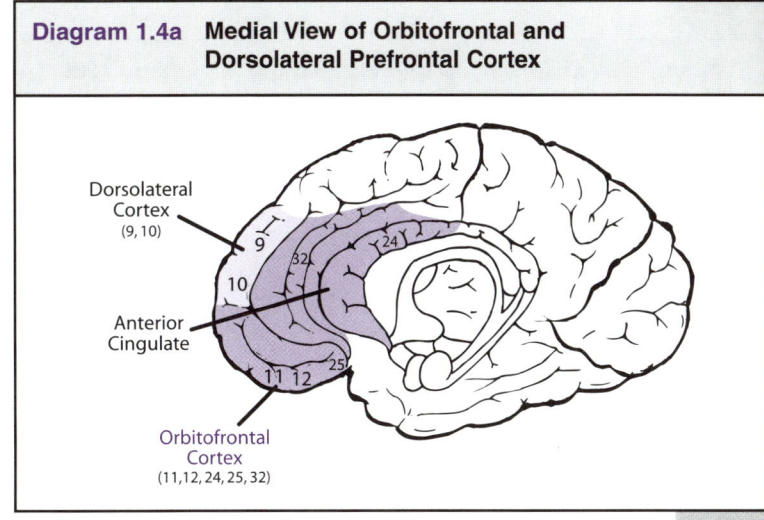

Diagram 1.4a Medial View of Orbitofrontal and Dorsolateral Prefrontal Cortex

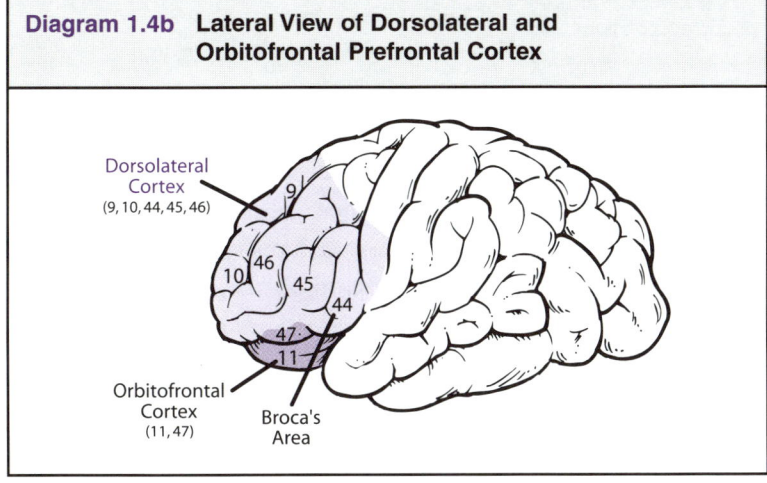

Diagram 1.4b Lateral View of Dorsolateral and Orbitofrontal Prefrontal Cortex

The paralimbic cortex is where the limbic cortex links to the prefrontal cortex and includes the anterior cingulate. The dorsolateral cortex is comprised of Brodmann's areas 9, 10, 44, 45, and 46 and occupies the anterior lateral surfaces of the frontal lobe.

The Source for Development of Executive Functions
Copyright © 2005 LinguiSystems, Inc.

Defining Executive Functions

Physiology of Executive Functions

Areas of the prefrontal cortex of the frontal lobe are delineated with specific responsibilities in executive functions. In general, the prefrontal cortex is primarily responsible for using processed information to make appropriate selections of movements and behaviors within a particular circumstance or situation. It receives information from a wide variety of other brain areas that is then used to prepare and anticipate appropriate actions.

Unidirectional and bi-directional neural connections exist between the prefrontal cortex and auditory, visual, and somatosensory association systems. Reciprocal connections also exist between the prefrontal cortex and thalamus, limbic system, reticular activating system, motor planning systems, and the cerebellum. Afferent networks bring representational information about the external environment from sensory association areas.

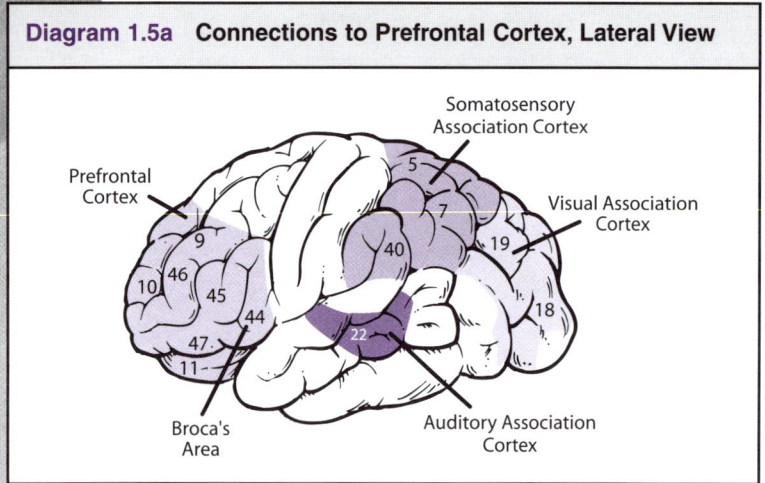

Diagram 1.5a Connections to Prefrontal Cortex, Lateral View

The limbic system provides input concerning the internal state of being, emotional representations, and motivational drives. Connections also link structures responsible for memory, allowing comparison with previous experiences to be factored into the prefrontal cortex decision-making processes. Links to the reticular activating system and hypothalamus provide for foundations of attention and arousal, upon which to begin higher-level processing. This combined set of input allows for weighing options to match a person's internal desires and previous experiences with the socially and culturally acceptable rules of the environment.

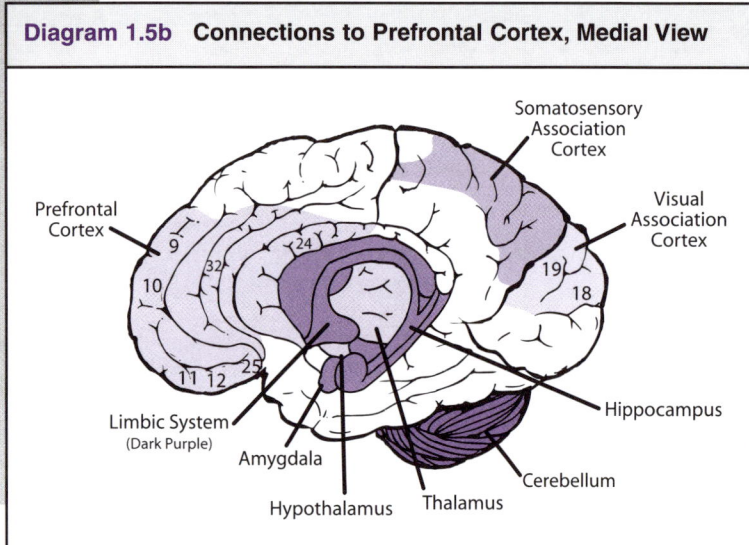

Diagram 1.5b Connections to Prefrontal Cortex, Medial View

The Source for Development of Executive Functions
Copyright © 2005 LinguiSystems, Inc.

Defining Executive Functions

A summary of information **received by the prefrontal cortex** includes:

- Sensory information from visual, auditory, and somatosensory cortical association zones about the external environment
- Information from the hypothalamus and reticular activating system about the internal state of the body
- Information from limbic system structures associated with motivation and affect

The prefrontal cortex must weigh all incoming information, compare it to previous experience and memory, mediate desires and emotions, and anticipate possible actions or goals to meet the demands of the environment. Efferent connections respond to lower-order association areas and to the motor system to coordinate, initiate, or inhibit relevant responses in the correct timing and sequence. Efferent connections also provide for ongoing monitoring and modulation of responses to meet the requirements for a situation and allow for adaptation and flexibility as necessary.

A summary of information **sent from the prefrontal cortex to other parts of the brain** includes:

- Association areas in the temporal, parietal, and occipital lobes
- Premotor region
- Limbic cortex and motor subcortical structures
- Subcortical structures such as the hypothalamus, thalamus, hippocampus, amygdala, and cerebellum

In addition, there are intraconnections within prefrontal structures that are linked to the remainder of the frontal lobe. The multiple networks allow the prefrontal cortex to plan and execute appropriate behavior based on incoming information, internal drives, emotional responses, and previous experience. Although it is difficult to specifically compartmentalize anatomical regions to isolated functions, there are some distinct patterns of performance that can be outlined.

Tables 1.3a, 1.3b, and 1.3c (pages 26-28) present an overview of brain-behavior correlates and functions of the prefrontal cortex.

Defining Executive Functions

Table 1.3a **Overview of Brain-Behavior Correlates and Functions of the Entire Prefrontal Cortex** (includes **orbitofrontal** and **dorsolateral** structures)

Prefrontal Connections	Prefrontal Functions	Effects of Delayed/ Disordered Development
With visual, auditory, and somatosensory cortical areas, subcortical motor systems, the limbic cortex, cerebellum, and intraconnections within the prefrontal cortex and frontal cortex	Serves as highest order of integration and association Controls flexible and adaptive behavior based on internal and external representations of world Serves as mechanism by which stored experiences are brought online to assist in planning and modifying behavior to meet requirements	Behavior disconnected from knowledge base, resulting in incoherent, fragmented, erratic behavior May display lack of initiative, inability to complete tasks to meet goals May demonstrate impulsive, hyper-expressive behaviors or behaviors inconsistent with plans and demands of environment or people May require significant external assistance, prompting, supervision May have poor academic, social, or vocational success

Defining Executive Functions

Table 1.3b **Specific Brain-Behavior Functions of the Orbitofrontal Prefrontal Cortex**
(sometimes further divided into **ventromedial** and **ventrolateral** areas)

Orbitofrontal Functions	Effects of Delayed/ Disordered Development
Makes decisions based on reward of eventual outcomes for long-term planning Selects and regulates appropriate responses and behaviors to meet plans	May make poor choices that do not reflect reasoning, experience, or awareness of consequences May be unable to delay gratification for better outcome; may exhibit impulsivity May demonstrate lack of concern for negative consequences of behavior and conduct; may lack good judgment
Has a role in self-regulation of behavior by inhibiting impulsive responses and drives and monitoring performance	Frequently exhibits impulsive and inappropriate behavior and communication, and poor self-control May be unable to restrain offensive, intrusive, inappropriate interactions with others Generally unable to follow social conventions Has difficulty completing tasks or assignments Lacks awareness of social gaffes and poor quality of work
Mediates affect and emotion	May be unable to integrate or express emotion
Incorporates past experiences and sensory input with internal impulses and emotions	May engage in offensive, inappropriate, risky behavior that does not reflect environmental input, past experience, or reasoning May make the same mistake repeatedly, failing to learn Unable to identify, regulate, or integrate emotion into decision making or social behavior choices

Defining Executive Functions

Table 1.3c **Specific Brain-Behavior Functions of the Dorsolateral Prefrontal Cortex**

Dorsolateral Functions	Effects of Delayed/ Disordered Development
Initiates, selects, and organizes relevant behaviors selected by the orbitofrontal prefrontal cortex	Has difficulty initiating activity May appear apathetic, indifferent, or withdrawn Initiates conversation or requests on a limited basis
Stores, updates, and manages verbal and visual working memory Sustains attention	Has difficulty maintaining attention to relevant information Exhibits distractibility or disrupted efforts Has trouble carrying out intended sequences given reduced working memory capacity
Provides temporal memory and organization Accesses episodic long-term memory	May be unable to retrieve memories for events in past, disrupting ability to compare to present circumstance May demonstrate a gap between verbal plans and motor behavior
Monitors, sequences, and modulates timing of relevant actions online	Has difficulty sequencing behaviors, plans, or language May be unable to end tasks appropriately May perseverate on behaviors beyond the point of usefulness
Makes inferences and decisions Evaluates outcomes and new-learning by association while engaged in task or behavior	May repeat errors or failed task strategies May take risks and break rules May contribute to the selection of inappropriate or non-advantageous goals and ineffective plans

Defining Executive Functions

The functional physiological aspects of executive functions described in the following section are based on functional magnetic resonance imaging (fMRI), positron emission tomography (PET), SPECT imaging, neuropsychological test profiles, clinical observations of neurological patients (case studies), neuroanatomical studies of cytoarchitecture, and neurophysiological studies from non-human primates. It is critical to understand that these divisions represent the most agreed upon functions of the areas listed. Different researchers define and study the functions of prefrontal cortex regions in different manners. Some look at global prefrontal function; others test or image very specific areas.

The **orbitofrontal** region is generally responsible for the inhibition of inappropriate impulses and desires and for decision making designed to meet beneficial long-term outcomes. Self-control, the ability to delay gratification, and emotional regulation are mediated here as well. This is the part of the brain that allows us to think before we speak and consider the consequences, both negative and positive, of our choices and actions. This part of the prefrontal cortex also plays a role in self-monitoring, such as recognizing the negative consequences of one's impulsive or emotionally-inappropriate behaviors. In cases of acquired lesions to this area of the prefrontal cortex, individuals are often observed to behave in a socially inappropriate manner. Their conversation might be characterized by "rude" comments. Drastic changes in personality are noted, with hyperactivity, hypersexuality, impulsiveness, irritability, or lability observed.

Children with delayed development in this area may be more impulsive in their responses and lack good judgment in their decision making. They may demonstrate responses to internal and external stimuli without regard for their actions, and lack empathy for another person. Adequate executive functions mediated by the orbitofrontal area of the prefrontal cortex would inhibit impulsive, reflexive responses and allow for generating planned interactions that are more acceptable in a given situation. The ability to behave in an "acceptable" manner in social, home, academic, and vocational environments is reliant on normal orbitofrontal development and functioning.

The **dorsolateral** area of the prefrontal cortex organizes complex behaviors based on plans selected by the orbitofrontal cortex. It accesses episodic long-term memory stores to retrieve knowledge from past experiences to assist in planning, sequencing, and organizing steps. Working memory provides a holding place for information so it can be accessed, coordinated, compared, and then used according to plan. Some aspects of sustained attention are also mediated here, as are temporal memory for the sequential order and frequency of events. Work in progress is monitored and modulated for timing and sequencing to meet an intended outcome. New learning and previous experiences add to the success or failure of task execution. In adults with acquired injuries to this part of the prefrontal cortex, the inability to initiate may be seen as apathy or indifference. Not only is initiation difficult, but the ability to terminate tasks when completed can also be observed (perseveration). Impaired temporal and spatial recall can limit a person's capacity for remembering what happened when and where.

Children with delayed development in this area of the prefrontal cortex may be inattentive, disorganized, and have difficulty starting and completing tasks in sequential order. They may be unable to generate a viable plan or realize when key steps are missing. Finishing work and moving from one assignment to another within a given time frame may be deficit. Limitations in working memory can impair their retention of directions and explanations. They may be slow to alter unsuccessful plans or strategies, or may repeatedly use ineffective strategies.

Summary

Executive functions are comprised of the ability to anticipate consequences, generate novel solutions, initiate appropriate actions or responses to situations, monitor the ongoing success or failure of one's behavior, and modify performance based on unexpected changes.

Executive functions are situated in the prefrontal cortex of the frontal lobe, the most recently evolved part of the human brain. The prefrontal cortex is involved in controlling behavior based on afferent input and efferent direction to nearly all other cortical and many subcortical brain structures.

The frontal lobe is comprised of the primary motor cortex, the premotor cortex, the supplementary motor cortex, Broca's area (motor speech), the frontal eye fields, and the prefrontal cortex. The prefrontal cortex lies just anterior to the premotor cortex.

The prefrontal cortex is linked to other parts of the frontal cortex, other posterior cortical structures, and many subcortical structures. These links are generally bi-directional, with afferent input arriving from the environment, memories from past experience, and current emotional and motivational states. Behaviors are then regulated via efferent connections to limbic, motor, and sensory association cortices. The process is highly complex, flexible, and simultaneous.

Defining Executive Functions

General brain-behavior correlates can be delineated in the prefrontal cortex. Orbitofrontal structures are typically engaged in the selection of goals based on outcomes, the inhibition of inappropriate responses, and the mediation and regulation of affect and drives. Choosing socially appropriate behavior and delaying impulsive needs for long-term gratification are also mediated here.

Dorsolateral structures generally are responsible for the initiation of behaviors, the sequencing and organization of efforts, and monitoring the success of these efforts. Working memory supports these efforts, as do systems of attention, temporal recall, and episodic long-term memory.

Children with delays in these neural systems display an array of behaviors that collectively can result in any combination of the following:

- Inattention to relevant incoming information
- Poor mediation of emotions
- Difficulty controlling impulsive behavior
- Deficits in organizing effective approaches to problem solving
- Repetition of past errors and difficulty learning from previous experience
- Inability to retain necessary information in working memory long enough to execute a task
- Poor behavioral transitions
- Socially inappropriate behavior

The Source for Development of Executive Functions
Copyright © 2005 LinguiSystems, Inc.

Chapter 2
Development of Executive Functions

Overview

The development of executive functions spans more years in the human lifetime than any other developmental sequence, including language, motor, and cognitive skills. This is largely due to the prolonged maturational phase of the frontal lobe, a process that begins in infancy and extends into early adulthood, before beginning an age-related decline in some individuals. A fully developed executive system allows us to comprehend subtle nuances in complex social situations and respond accordingly to constantly changing social, academic, and vocational demands. Once fully developed, executive functions provide us with a measure of self-control and the ability to make good long-term decisions and to behave within the parameters of society, given the quality of our underlying cognition, language, motor, and perceptual functioning. Mature executive functions allow for the "growing up" of an individual.

The frontal lobe is the most recently evolved part of the human brain and is responsible for the most complex integration of information from all other parts of the cortex and subcortical structures. The evolution of the prefrontal cortex with its executive functions is considered by some to be the source of what makes us truly human. As the prefrontal neural networks develop, we become better at adapting to changing circumstances, engaging in goal-directed behaviors, and making ethical, moral, or legal decisions without sabotaging our efforts with impulsivity or poor choices. Some theorists in the area of social cognition define the highest order of human altruism as a level of being socially aware and committed to working toward the better good of all people (Kane & Engle 2002).

The complexity of this metacognitive system relies on the complete development of intricate connections throughout the brain, as well as the maturation of other neural systems and the frontal lobe; but the process of getting there is a long one. Becoming a fully participating member of society, no matter what culture we find ourselves in, is a long journey. Most parents can relate to the utter frustration of trying to corral an impulsive two-year-old who tries to run out into the street with no apparent awareness of danger. Now think about a four-year-old who is better able to control some impulses and has a longer attention span, but still melts down with tears due to the inability to delay gratification for a long-term outcome. Twelve-year-olds are better yet at sustaining attention and can make reasonable plans and solve some complex problems, but they do not yet have the strategic thinking required for the kind of planning and goal-directed behavior required of an adult trying to navigate the ups and downs of life. By the time we reach young adulthood, it is assumed that we have developed the wisdom to productively engage in meaningful aspects of life—work, family, home, and community—without undermining the outcome with inaccurate

Development of Executive Functions

social judgments or poorly formed goals. Hopefully, we live a productive life before beginning to experience an age-related decline in decision making, judgment, insight, and problem solving—all of which can make us dependent once again on family assistance to maintain independence.

As with any other developmental sequence, it is important to understand how and when executive functions come online. Accurate assessment and identification of deficits in executive functions cannot be completed without first understanding normal development. Treatment plans must take into account the typical developmental sequences for executive functions, similar to treatment plans for language or motor deficits. Professionals providing remediation for executive function disorders in children need to understand what degree of skill should be expected at various ages. Treatment plans should include those components of executive function that are missing from the child's developmental profile.

The maturation of this complex network of higher order neural pathways is twofold: there is an underlying continuous progression of frontal lobe development and maturation, upon which is superimposed multistage spurts of high-intensity development of different components of executive functions at various ages. Each stage of development contributes an ever-increasing ability to manage more complex and variable problems, as well as the ability to integrate more abstract language as a means of verbally mediating performance.

The development of cognitive, linguistic, sensory, and motor functions are a by-product of the maturation and myelination of brain regions; the same can be said for the development of executive functions. As cognitive processes improve and executive functions come online, there is an increase in the ability to function independently in situations requiring adaptation and self-monitoring. Some researchers (Thatcher 1991, Anderson 2001) suggest a link between the normal acquisition of executive functions with Piaget's stages of cognitive development, finding similarities in the bursts of growth at different ages (e.g., sensorimotor period). Other theorists (Anderson 2002) package similar executive skills together into contextualized groups (e.g., cognitive flexibility or attentional control) and discuss the development of executive functions in this fashion.

It is also important to remember that development of any skill can be divided into the following three stages:

1. **Emerging**—early acquisition and not yet functional
2. **Developing**—partially acquired capacity but not fully functional
3. **Established**—fully mature and functional

Development of Executive Functions

The development of executive functions is not a clear linear track. It is important to understand that various aspects or components of executive function come into maturity at different times. There also appears to be some prerequisite developmental skills that are necessary as a foundation for executive functions. At the same time, the general continual process of neural maturation of the frontal lobe is ongoing. Despite the perceived complexity, it is possible to describe a general developmental pattern that is typical for executive functions. In the following sections, various aspects of development for executive functions are explained, including general frontal lobe development.

Frontal Lobe Development

Maturation of frontal lobe connections to other parts of the brain is required for the development of normal executive functions. The frontal lobe must form links with the rest of the brain through myelinization, synaptic connections, and pruning in order to develop mature neurological networks. This process starts at birth and extends into adulthood, which is a much slower rate of maturation when compared to the rest of the cerebrum. For example, myelination begins at birth but does not terminate until the mid-twenties. Synaptic density reaches its peak between the ages of one and two, at which point the long processes of synaptic pruning begins. *Pruning*—the process by which weaker synapses are actually *deleted* to promote better efficiency and efficacy of synaptic networks—accounts for the loss of about half of our synapses by puberty. Pruning is affected by both our environment and experiences, which literally shape the nature of early network development.

Adult levels of synaptic density and network development are not reached until mid-adolescence and do not fully stabilize until the early twenties. It is not until mid-adulthood that the number of neurons begins to slowly decline. This lengthy arc of maturation of the frontal lobes is the main reason that young children lack judgment, abstract reasoning, and the capacity for insight. Adolescents are in a relatively better position to anticipate outcomes and make long-term plans, however the neural networks required for wise decision making are not completely stable until early adulthood.

A general timeline of the development of frontal lobe functions is presented in Table 2.1 (page 35).

Development of Executive Functions

Table 2.1 Timeline for Normal Development of Frontal Lobe Functions

Age	Description
In utero	• Frontal lobe fissures last to develop
At birth	• Prefrontal neurons still immature • Minimal electrical activity in prefrontal cortex • Myelination begins and extends throughout adulthood
6-12 months	• Metabolic activity in orbitofrontal gyrus (begins to assume *some* control over emotions) increases steadily until 4 years of age • Increased glucose use, massive dendritic growth, and beginning of myelination from frontal lobe to limbic system • Myelination between frontal lobe and limbic system (for emotional development) continues well into adolescence • Myelination between frontal lobe and medial temporal lobes (for memory networks) begins around 9 months
1-2 years	• Frontal lobe sulci completely formed by 1 year • Dendrites fully extended and synapses reach maximum density by 2 years • Prefrontal cells begin long stage of synaptic pruning, continuing into adolescence
3-6 years	• Peak growth rates in communication between hemispheres
7-10 years	• Accelerated development of frontal regions in general • Fine tuning of neural connections results in improved self-control and operational thinking • Synaptic density begins to decline until about 16 years, when adult level attained
10-12 years	• Systems of inhibition and strategy development mature, resulting in improved problem solving and improved efficiency and quality of strategies
Adolescence	• Adult level of synaptic density reached at about 16 years • Continued changes in metabolic and electrical activity
Mid-20s	• Myelination of frontal lobe neurons tapers off • Neural connections and syntactic density stabilize, with an increase in abstract thinking and long-range planning
Early adulthood	• Enhanced goal selection and attainment for personal expansion, identity, independence, and achievement
Mid-adulthood	• Number of neurons relatively constant until around age 45, at which point there is a slow decline
Late adulthood	• Amount of information that can be stored in working memory decreases • Possible decrease in abstract reasoning and judgment may lead to age-related decline in independent life skills

adapted from Anderson (2001); Eliot (1999)

Development of Executive Functions

Executive Function Development

Executive functions emerge and mature at different stages. There are multiple spurts of intense development and maturation, beginning at birth and extending through early adulthood. This means that some skills may be emerging while others are nearing maturity. These developmental spurts are superimposed over the underlying, ongoing process of frontal lobe maturation. The degree to which executive functions mature in an individual is dependent upon the completion and successful myelination of the frontal lobe, the integrity of other cortical and subcortical functions, environmental influences, and cultural variables.

It is important to understand that the effectiveness of higher order integration systems is dependent upon the quality of incoming information—"Garbage in, garbage out," so to speak. Sensory association areas must provide complete and accurate information from the environment to the prefrontal cortex. Incoming information about emotional states and motivation in a given situation must be readily available for integration with incoming perceptual information. Memory systems provide long-term storage of information from which to draw upon when using executive functions to learn from experience. Language is used to assist the individual with self-analysis of the actions chosen.

Attention and inhibition are thought to provide a foundation for the development of working memory. Working memory, along with the capacity to attend and inhibit impulses, allows for the use and manipulation of increasingly longer strings of information. Being able to attend to relevant information and inhibit impulsive behaviors or reactions allows for better goal-selection, planning, organization, and self-monitoring. An individual cannot solve a problem, make comparisons, juggle multiple factors, or plan for long-term outcomes effectively if attention wanders, distractions interfere, or working memory is insufficient to hold the requirements of the situation in store long enough to form and execute a plan.

Executive functions must proceed through their own developmental phases in order to effectively mediate and modify responses to the environment. The main spurts of intense development for executive functions take place at three critical age levels: 5-7 years, 9-12 years, and adolescence, with maturity being attained in the early 20s. Because different skill sets emerge and mature at different ages, it is difficult to present a simple timeline of this process. Anderson (2002) presents a model of executive function development that classifies specific executive skills into four groups of multiple-process systems: attentional control, information processing, cognitive flexibility, and goal setting. Table 2.2 (page 37) presents conceptual definitions of Anderson's model of executive functions.

Development of Executive Functions

Table 2.2 Model of Executive Function Domains (Anderson 2002)

System	Definition/Description
Attentional- and Self-Control	• Focuses, sustains, and selectively attends to information relevant to current and long-term requirements • Inhibits ineffective or destructive responses long enough to process, plan, and execute appropriate behaviors • Controls impulsivity, via internal or external cues, in order to carry out task demands within given environment
Information Processing	• Sensory input processed with fluency, speed, and efficiency • Quality and quantity of processed information affects ultimate quality of outcome • Performance and behavior dependent on integration of primary and association systems with tertiary processing • Language processing skills used to internally mediate plans and efforts (e.g., self-talk)
Flexible, Purposeful Behavior	• Shifts between different sets as required for different responses • Divides attention between multiple or changing demands • Simultaneously processes multiple sources of incoming information • Generates alternative or multiple strategies • Learns from mistakes • Adapts to changing circumstances in timely manner
Goal Setting and Achievement	• Ability to anticipate outcomes and predict consequences blended with current situational demands • Calls up previously learned routines, if appropriate • Generates goals and plans for novel situations • Initiates work on tasks in efficient, organized manner • Works within given parameters to meet outcomes, whether self-determined or externally-driven • Applies self-monitoring skills to successfully meet goals

Development of Executive Functions

Grouping executive functions in this way can provide some structure and order to the complex task of understanding the maturation of specific executive function skills at different times. Components of executive functions and cognitive processes can be embedded into the four domains listed in Table 2.2 (page 37). This grouping simplifies the task of trying to identify deficit areas and focus treatment objectives.

The following section provides tables that outline the general developmental phases of these four skill areas. Note the age ranges for critical spurts of maturation. While some skills begin to emerge as early as infancy and toddlerhood, surges of development in other areas tend to occur around the age of 5 years, then again from 9-12 years, and once again in adolescence. We should emphasize that the current research available for development of executive functions does not yet provide a "tidy" outline that matches exact ages with exact skills. These tables provide a starting point from which to build an understanding of how different executive functions come online and mature at different times.

Table 2.3a Attentional- and Self-Control by Age

Age	Attentional- and Self-Control (impulse control and self-inhibition as the fundamental groundwork for all goal-directed, planned behavior)
6-12 months	• Early inhibitory control emerges, although still generally unable to inhibit previously learned responses • Can tolerate longer delays and still maintain simple, focused attention
1-2 years	• As early as 1 year, can inhibit certain behaviors and shift to new response sets • Some self-monitoring and early ability to identify errors, but these skills are inconsistent • No self-correction of any errors that may have been identified • Impulsive behaviors reflect immature attentional system, distractibility, and undeveloped inhibitory control
3-6 years	• Continued, general increases in attention, self-control, concentration, and inhibition, but not yet mature • Gradual decline in impulsivity, although still present • Occasional perseverative behavior • At age 6, ability to resist distractions and maintain attention begins to increase
7-9 years	• Selective attention (ability to attend to relevant stimuli while tuning out competing/distracting stimuli) beginning to develop and mature • Significant improvement in ability to inhibit impulsive actions between 9 and 12 years

continued on next page

Development of Executive Functions

Table 2.3a, continued Attentional- and Self-Control by Age

Age	Attentional- and Self-Control (impulse control and self-inhibition as the fundamental groundwork for all goal-directed, planned behavior)
10 years	• Selective attention nearing maturity; better able to selectively attend to relevant and necessary information in environment • Control of impulses may begin to reach adult levels of performance
11-12 years	• Able to monitor and regulate actions well • Relative maturity of attentional functions • Able to limit perseverative errors at adult level • Temporary increase in impulsivity for short periods
Adolescence	• Perseverative errors rare • Working memory increases significantly

adapted from Anderson (2002); Zelazo & Mueller (2002); Anderson (2001); Welsh, Pennington, & Grossier (1991); Miller & Weiss (1981) as cited in Passler, Isaac, & Hynd (1985); Eliot (1999); Anderson et al. (2001); Levin et al. (1991) as cited in Brocki & Bohlin (2004).

Table 2.3b Information Processing by Age

Age	Information Processing (necessary for blending language and working memory with previous experience to assist in determining plans or selecting appropriate behaviors)
3-5 years	• Incremental improvements in verbal fluency • Gradual improvements in processing speed and accuracy on impulse control tasks • 4-year-olds able to process 2- and 3-step units of information • 5-year-olds able to process 4-step units of information
6-7 years	• Begin to use silent, verbal mediation as language becomes more complex • 6-year-olds able to process up to 5-step "moves" in simple problem solving
9-12 years	• Continued improvement in processing speed and fluency • Significant gains in processing speed • Verbal fluency near maturity
Adolescence	• Increased verbal fluency and sequencing • Continued improvements in both efficiency and fluency of information processing • Incremental improvements minimal from age 15 on

adapted from Anderson (2002); Klahr & Robinson (1981) as cited in Zelazo & Mueller (2002)

Development of Executive Functions

Table 2.3c Cognitive Flexibility and Purposeful Behavior by Age

Age	Cognitive Flexibility and Purposeful Behavior (adaptability necessary for meeting social, community, and academic demands)
Infancy	• Behavior is more reflexive and perseverative in nature and designed to meet immediate needs • Cognitive flexibility not yet emerged
18-24 months	• Begin to identify correct versus incorrect block constructions (compared to designs) but unable to actually shift approach to "fix" incorrect version
2-4 years	• 2 ½-year-olds demonstrate knowledge of rules but unable to shift or alter behaviors, demonstrating perseveration • 3-year-olds demonstrate knowledge of rules and emerging ability to shift behaviors accordingly, but only for *one* rule necessary for task success • 4-year-olds begin to demonstrate ability to shift and flex between two simple task requirements, but continue to have difficulty when response sets increase in complexity • 4-year-olds begin to have more successful task completion due to increase in mental flexibility and rapid switching between two simple response sets
5-6 years	• 5-year-olds demonstrate difficulty switching between multiple rules, even when verbal cues are given • Spurt of development in mental flexibility around 6 years • Decline in perseverative behavior • Emerging capacity to learn from mistakes and create alternative strategies for simple problems
7-9 years	• 7-year-olds struggle with switching behavior sets that are contingent on multiple demands • 8-year-olds demonstrate increase in focused, sustained, and shifting attention • 9-year-olds begin to have more success switching rules/sets between multiple or changing demands
10-12 years	• Ability to switch between multiple task demands continues to improve, with concomitant decline in perseverative, non-task oriented behaviors • Increasing capacity to learn from mistakes and devise alternative strategies for more complicated and multi-dimensional problems
Adolescence	• Relative maturation of cognitive flexibility • Perseverative behavior (not task-oriented performance) rare • Flexibility to switch between changing performance demands and initiate deliberate behaviors much improved

adapted from Anderson, P. (2002); Diamond & Goldman-Rakic (1989) as cited in Anderson, V. (2001); Passler, Isaac, & Hynd (1985); Anderson et al. (2001); Rebok et al. (1997) as cited in Klenberg, Korkman, & Lahti-Nuuttila (2001)

Development of Executive Functions

Table 2.3d	Goal Setting and Achievement by Age
Age	**Goal Setting and Achievement** (self-awareness within context of other people and external requirements, prediction of outcomes, and purposeful behavior)
3 years	• Difficulty organizing plans and actions • Difficulty with conceptual reasoning • Use inefficient or fragmented strategies • Make disadvantageous choices and choices by chance • Less able to delay gratification
4-5 years	• 4-year-olds begin to make more advantageous choices • 4-year-olds capable of generating new concepts and ideas • 4- to 5-year-olds begin to delay initial choices for behavior, selecting goals that lead to "better" rewards later on • Simple strategic planning skills emerge • Make better choices (more advantageous and less by chance)
6 years	• Demonstrate more frequent strategic and planned goal choices and behaviors, but not yet mastered
7-10 years	• Rapid surge in development of planning and organizational skills that reflect consideration of task parameters more so than personal or impulsive desires • Strategic behavior and efficient reasoning become more obvious
11-13 years	• Developmental spurt for goal-setting skills around 12 years • Increased ability to use strategies for problem solving • Complex planning skills nearing maturity • 12-year-olds may demonstrate adult levels of planning abilities and performance of planned behavior
Adolescence	• Increase in more complex planning and organizational skills • Strategy development and its use in complex, multidimensional goal-oriented behavior continues to improve • Overall skills in decision making, goal selection, and capacity to orchestrate efforts necessary to attain goals continue to improve

adapted from Anderson, P. (2002); Chelune & Baer (1986) as cited in Anderson, V. (2001); Welsh, Pennington, & Grossier (1991); Zelazo & Mueller (2002)

Development of Executive Functions

Attentional control skills appear to reach maturity before more complex processes such as cognitive flexibility or goal setting. Tremendous gains in development occur between birth and five years of age, which correspond to the first significant growth spurt in the frontal lobe. It is important to understand how critical attention is to the overall success of executive functions for processing, organizing, planning, and executing tasks well. Without attention, it is difficult to be in a state of readiness to receive and attend to relevant stimuli. Without attention, we cannot adequately plan or carry out steps over a period of time. Without attention, we cannot begin to monitor the success or failure of efforts, and distractions are more likely to interfere with behaviors.

Information processing skills demonstrate a surge in development between 9 and 12 years of age. By adolescence, children are able to process with greater speed and accuracy and are likely to be better suited for managing multiple streams of incoming information. Accurate perceptions of the environment—whether visual or auditory, simple or complex—are a must. The quality of information sent forward to the prefrontal cortex for integration and decision making directly affects the appropriateness of plans and goals. How well we integrate our emotions with requirements and demands from the environment has a direct impact on whether we choose appropriate behaviors and words.

Cognitive flexibility skills also demonstrate spurts of development in the ability to shift and manage changing demands. Whereas basic processing and comparison of environmental input requires simple sustained attention, the ability to shift between changing sets of information and demands relies on shifting attention accordingly. The capacity to make these changes, or demonstrate cognitive flexibility in thinking and planning, is required for behavioral adaptation. We cannot adapt to the environment (select new goals, develop alternative plans, stop using ineffective strategies) without fluently switching between incoming information and environmental requirements or limitations.

Goal-setting skills can mature once the individual develops the ability to attend to relevant input, process and organize information accurately and quickly, and then shift with the changing tide of internal emotions and external requirements. Developing complex strategies and making decisions based on anticipation of outcomes and long-term goals also require the simultaneous manipulation of multiple variables. The ability to reason conceptually assists in planning for the future.

Development of Executive Functions

The development of executive functions is dependent upon many factors and occurs in spurts from childhood through adolescence, before stabilizing in early adulthood. The development of executive function skills is thought to mirror Piaget's stages of cognitive development, which are discussed in the next section.

Cognitive Development

Cognitive development must be adequately accomplished to achieve the "metacognitive" level necessary for well developed executive function abilities. *Metacognitive* means that an individual knows what she knows and understands what she needs to know in order to learn. Table 2.4 summarizes Piaget's developmental stages.

Table 2.4 Piaget's Stages of Cognitive Development

Piagetian Stage	Age	Description
Sensorimotor	Birth-2 years	Pre-symbolic; pre-speech; knowledge coded by sensory-motor action
Preoperational	2-7 years	Centration and irreversibility; classification through symbols; knowledge coded by how things appear
Concrete Operational	7-11 years	Decentering and reversibility; retain basic qualities beyond appearance; knowledge coded through mental manipulation of symbols to re-present information
Formal Operational	11-16 years	Engage in logical, hypothetical, inferential thinking

The first stage of cognitive development is the **sensorimotor stage**. At this stage, a child acquires knowledge and solves problems in the environment by acting on them through motor activity. If the child wants an item, she goes to it and manipulates it through sensory-motor interaction with the item. The child learns through what she can directly experience. This is a very concrete, factual level of thinking that exists during a pre-speech phase of development. The child is not able to verbally express what she is thinking or desiring, so she acts on it. The language generated during this stage is primarily to label or name things. This phase of cognitive development is very behavioral, based in concrete action and exploration.

Development of Executive Functions

The second stage of cognitive development is called the **preoperational stage**. A child is very appearance oriented in this phase, exploring how things look, taste, feel, smell, and taste. A symbolic representation emerges, in which a child can understand that something can represent an object, such as a picture representing the actual item. The child begins to classify items by their perceptual traits, such as color, size, and shape. However, knowledge and symbolic representation is still based around the child's experiences (centration) and interaction with the object in its present state (irreversibility). While cognition begins to engage in symbolic representation in beginning levels of abstraction, it is still grounded in interaction with objects and the environment. The child begins to engage in symbolic play and is able to transform something into what is desired, but perception is still dominant over reasoning.

The third Piagetian developmental phase is the **concrete operational stage**. During this stage, a child learns to mentally manipulate symbols to represent information. They can understand that how something looks doesn't mean it has changed; it will retain its basic qualities (reversibility). For example, looking at a picture of something doesn't mean that the item became flat; the child can reverse the actual image in her mind to more accurately represent it mentally. The child also becomes able to retain basic qualities of items she might not have experienced personally (decentering). The child in this stage is less egocentric and begins to reason logically and to classify information using more abstract features, such as analysis of similarities and differences.

The last stage of cognitive development is the **formal operational stage**. At this stage, a child begins to use deductive reasoning skills. Knowledge is expanded by formulating a hypothesis and then generating possibilities to test for a solution. Thinking is now based in symbols and ideas rather than actual objects. Abstract concepts, such as distance, time, space, and probability, all become part of cognition. This type of thinking process is often referred to as the *scientific method*. The child is able to infer new ideas from previous knowledge and then map a strategy to determine if her thought process is accurate.

Piaget's stages of cognitive development are well known and typically included in most child development courses. However, Piaget also mapped out affective development in those same stages and age levels. His construct for affective development is more congruent with the control over behavior applied by executive functions, in that our prefrontal cortex compares internal drives with external requirements and then mediates an appropriate response. Impulses must be inhibited; emotional perspectives must be recognized and accounted for, both of the individual and those with whom she is interacting.

Development of Executive Functions

The following section re-examines Piaget's stages with a focus on affective development. Table 2.5 presents a summary of this information.

Table 2.5 Piaget's Stages of Affective Development		
Piagetian Stage	**Age**	**Description**
Sensorimotor	Birth-2 years	Acquire feelings; invest affection in others
Preoperational	2-7 years	Reciprocity and moral feelings
Concrete Operational	7-11 years	Cooperation; conservation of feelings and values; mutual respect; will and autonomy
Formal Operational	11-16 years	Personality formation; idealistic feelings

During the **sensorimotor stage**, a child transitions from the instinctive reflexive drives and reactions into feeling emotion. Feelings of contentment and pleasure can be linked to actions, such as drinking a bottle or getting a clean diaper. Those feelings begin to expand into emotions, such as joy, sorrow, and disappointment. However, the self and environment are still connected at this stage, so the child's affect is centered around self. As motor skills improve and the child can interact with the environment more directly from 1-2 years of age, affect expands into emotions of success and failure, based on the child's actions. The child also begins to invest certain emotions and reactions in specific people, such as the caregivers and siblings. Emotions, such as liking and disliking, emerge at the same time as the child becomes more consciously social with definite preferences. Moral concepts and rules have not developed at this stage, thus we refer to the "terrible twos" as children engage in what they want to do and don't respond to "no!"

The first social feelings develop during the **preoperational stage**. Language development plays a part because for the first time the child has words to represent emotions. The child can also recall and remember the emotions and use language to reconstruct the cognitive images that triggered a feeling. Behavior also becomes more stable and predictable during this phase, leading to increased reciprocity in interaction. The child's social development is marked by "remembering" the feelings associated with specific interactions. Value judgments become attached to anticipating positive feelings when interacting with someone

The Source for Development of Executive Functions
Copyright © 2005 LinguiSystems, Inc.

Development of Executive Functions

and avoiding a replication of negative feelings from an unpleasant interaction. This leads toward the development of the first moral feelings. Concepts of compliance with rules, lying, and justice evolve, accompanied by intention and accidents. While still primarily egocentric, the child begins to make decisions based on the feelings that result from her actions.

Cognitive and affective development become inseparable at the **concrete operational stage**. The reversibility cognitive skill that emerges has a great impact on affect. A child develops the ability to conserve feelings and values from one event to another. Past feelings can now play a part in reasoning through social situations. The child also develops a "will," which is a set of values that the individual feels obliged to follow. The concept of having an "obligation" to behave in a certain way and the realization that she is responsible for the self-regulation of her own behavior leads to a sense of autonomy within the individual; she is responsible for governing her own actions. The child's efforts toward learning to self-regulate lead to a concept of mutual respect and cooperation. The self-regulation applies to the child herself as well as other people; it is a cooperative effort on everyone's part. This realization plays into further understanding of intentionality and capability to consider motives and make judgments regarding people's actions.

The emergence of the ability to hypothetically reason during the **formal operational stage** of development leads to the metacognitive skills mentioned at the beginning of this section, page 43. The child begins to reflect on her own thinking or can think about thinking. While the child tends to be somewhat egocentric in her reasoning, with increased age and experience she begins to gain an appreciation of the world at large. The initial stages of metacognitive development tend to be very idealistic as a result. The second aspect of affective development during this phase is development of a value system, using the components of will and autonomy from the concrete operational stage. The child changes from her focus on self to a personality that is oriented toward the social world, based on a desire to fit in. The idealistic viewpoint begins to temper as the child becomes more realistic and recognizes the need to adapt to society and the real world. Piaget defines *personality* as the result of the autonomous individual's efforts to adapt to the social world of adults.

The outline of Piaget's affective development delineates stages for developing problem solving skills, the ability to inhibit undesirable responses and anticipate consequences, and the ability to recognize and act on important social cues present in the external environment. These skills are mediated by executive functions and become more complex as the prefrontal cortex develops.

Development of Executive Functions

Development of Self-Control

As children grow, they begin to demonstrate increased control over appropriate social judgment and behavior. *Emotional intelligence* can be defined as the ability to recognize and control one's own feelings, as well as the ability to read and respond to the feelings of others. The development of emotional intelligence plays a significant part in determining later success in various developmental areas, but especially in the area of social cognition. Research has shown that children who demonstrate good impulse control at the age of four years achieved higher SAT scores later in life. In addition, these individuals were better socially adapted teenagers; they got along better with other people and demonstrated more dependable interactions.

Wood (2003) provides an executive function correlate for the development of social cognition. As mentioned in Chapter 1, pages 21-25, certain limbic structures, connected to the medial frontal and orbitofrontal portions of the prefrontal cortex, mediate and regulate emotional intelligence—that is, the ability to identify and regulate one's own emotions and to recognize and respond appropriately to the emotions and circumstances of others. Wood identified various parameters of social cognition, including the following:

- Self-control of aggression and violence
- Social behavior
- Social perception and judgment
- Mental state representation
- Social decision making

Networks that process self-control are one of the slowest to develop, as they require fully myelinated limbic structures and frontal lobe structures. But once intact, connections between the amygdala via the limbic system to the orbitofrontal prefrontal cortex allow refinement of skills required to regulate social behavior. Those skills can include the following:

- Processing emotions, such as fear and happiness
- Evaluating the emotional significance of an event to determine an appropriate social response
- Identifying threats and an aggressive response, if needed
- Processing visual features and the emotional significance of facial expressions

Development of Executive Functions

- Generating emotional facial expression
- Forming mental representations of others' perspectives
- Evaluating the emotional significance of rewards or consequences of social decisions
- Making advantageous social decisions for long-term rewards
- Engaging in moral reasoning

These skills allow individuals to minimize disruptive or injurious behavior and engage in conflict resolution when necessary.

Summary

The development of the frontal lobe is a continuous, lengthy process; longer than any other developmental phase. Executive function development is superimposed onto the continuous myelinization and synaptic pruning of the frontal lobe. Executive functions develop in multiple stages with growth spurts occurring between 5-7 years, 9-12 years, and in adolescence. Stability of executive functions occurs in early adulthood.

Components of executive functions can be grouped into four domains:

- Attentional control
- Information processing
- Cognitive flexibility
- Goal setting

Executive functions depend upon the integrity and development of language, perceptual skills, memory, and emotional processing. Environmental influence also plays a role in the development of executive skills. There are similarities between the stages of development and maturation of executive functions and the stages of cognitive development outlined by Piaget. Similarities also exist between the development of self-control and regulation (a component of executive functions) and Piaget's stages of affective development. The ability to participate successfully in social situations and to achieve long-term outcomes is highly dependent upon the normal development of executive functions.

Chapter 3
Co-Morbidity of Executive Functions with Other Disorders

Overview

Medical and educational professionals are beginning to diagnose "Executive Function Disorder." While an individual may have trouble with executive functions, it is somewhat erroneous to label that as the primary disorder. Difficulty organizing, integrating information, and responding appropriately occurs across a broad spectrum of disorders. However, the problems that occur in executive functions are secondary. They are caused by, or result from, the primary disorder.

Let's use a medical example to illustrate this idea.

> A child complains of a sore throat. You can do things to ease the tender throat, such as drinking tea with honey or eating ice cream, but the symptom is secondary to an infection. The child has strep throat, and the primary condition must be acknowledged to account for the symptom of the sore throat. The sore throat still needs to be addressed, but in the context of the bigger issue.
>
> Another example might be a child who is diagnosed as being selectively mute. The fact that the child is choosing not to talk is secondary to some other primary problem, such as a language disorder, phonological deficit, or emotional trauma. While the mutism needs to be addressed, it is symptomatic of a larger disability.

In adults, challenges in the area of executive functions are often the result of injury or trauma, such as a stroke or head injury. The individual previously used appropriate executive function skills but now struggles with these tasks after experiencing some other medical incident. In adults, problems in executive functions are usually considered to be an acquired disorder.

Children must develop executive functions as they grow and mature. If they fail to do so, it is usually because of something else that is interfering, such as a learning disability, autism, closed-head injury, language disorder, or medical syndrome. To label "Executive Function Disorder" as the stand-alone disability implies that all aspects of development are normal and no other problems are evidenced to account for the discrepancies in the individual's ability to integrate appropriately into the world. It is rather unusual for that to be the case; there is usually another disability that accounts for the deficits in executive functions. A secondary symptom should not be diagnosed as the primary disability.

Co-Morbidity of Executive Functions with Other Disorders

However, the skills encompassed under executive functions are critical for effective daily functioning and need to be part of the treatment goals for individuals with a variety of disorders.

There is no one global profile of executive function deficits. Rather, there exist different potential combinations of deficits that may manifest themselves in strikingly different ways, depending on the type of injury or atypical developmental pattern. In the population of individuals with an acquired injury to the prefrontal cortex, deficits can vary from being unable to initiate any behaviors to being unable to inhibit impulsive and hyper-expressed behaviors. Some individuals display inappropriate social behavior that is uncharacteristic to their previous personality. Adults (or children) with an acquired trauma to the frontal lobe may have difficulty organizing, sequencing, initiating, completing, or monitoring tasks. They may have difficulty keeping their impulses in check, or in being flexible. There are any number of combinations of possible deficits that can arise in the area of executive function skills. It is an oversimplification to say that all individuals who have deficits in executive functions will present in the same fashion.

> One of the most highly publicized and earliest documented case of frontal lobe injury was to a man by the name of Phineas Gage, a dynamite worker on a railroad in 1868. Mr. Gage was struck in the left frontal lobe, from the medial orbital region upward, with an iron bar during an explosion. Although he survived the accident, Mr. Gage's personality was described to have undergone significant changes following the accident. Before the accident, he had been responsible and capable of executing tasks; afterward he was often profane, impatient, obstinate, disagreeable, and unable to execute the many plans he attempted to start.

Other types of injuries to the frontal lobe may result in dramatically different deficits. Some individuals may demonstrate an extreme inability to initiate responses, to the extent that they require physical, hand-over-hand assistance in order to begin movement, even for routine or simple tasks, such as tying their shoes or writing their name. These individuals rarely initiate conversations or requests. Families are often perplexed at such significant changes in their loved ones' personalities and frustrated by their loss of ability to function independently. Therapy for these individuals must focus on addressing the specific deficit executive function skills that are present in conjunction with that injury. Specifically designed compensatory strategies, combined with work to increase self-awareness and regulation, can then offer the best opportunity for the individual with acquired executive function impairments to resume a degree of functional independence.

Co-Morbidity of Executive Functions with Other Disorders

Many children with atypical development of executive functions also fail to develop effective communication or social skills and may demonstrate behavioral problems due to impulsivity, limited self-control, disorganization, and inattention. The severity of these deficits in children has a high correlation with the success they achieve in academic settings and life as they mature. Just as the deficits resulting from an injury to the prefrontal cortex can vary, deficit executive function skills in children with atypical development are rarely homogenous.

Research in the past several years continues to identify more childhood developmental disorders with components of executive function deficits. Although specific patterns of executive function deficits cannot be identified and linked to particular developmental disorders, there are common characteristics in some disorders, such as attention deficit hyperactivity disorder (ADHD), Asperger's syndrome, or autistic spectrum disorders. For example, the inflexibility, impulsivity, and inattention inherent in ADHD contribute to inappropriate or unsuccessful social, behavioral, and communicative skills. Children with autistic spectrum disorders tend to present with deficits in other executive function skills, such as inflexibility and perseveration in behavior patterns.

One final point to make is that the relationship between executive function deficits and childhood disorders of communication, social interaction, and behavior, is unclear. There is no definitive agreement as to whether atypical patterns in prefrontal cortical development and concomitant executive function deficits are an underlying **cause** of the disorder, a **result** of the disorder, or a **co-existing symptomatic presentation** of the disorder. The most current, and rational, approach is to address deficit executive function skills as a symptomatic presentation of these disorders. One thing is certain—without looking at the relationship between communication, behavior, and executive function skills, it is likely that intervention will be less successful in transitioning to learning environments, therefore limiting the ultimate success of the child to achieve his potential.

The remainder of this chapter will discuss several developmental disorders and the components of executive function deficits associated with each of them. The disorders addressed are not an exhaustive list of possible co-morbid conditions. Instead, they are included to illustrate the manner in which executive function skills are frequently compromised within a variety of developmental disorders that occur in children.

Co-Morbidity of Executive Functions with Other Disorders

Autism and Executive Functions

Autism is a developmental syndrome disorder characterized by impairments in the following areas:

- Reciprocal social interaction
- Verbal and nonverbal communication
- Behavior, resulting in restricted, repetitive, stereotypic patterns

Onset of deficits in these three defined areas occurs during the developmental period and differences are evidenced by three years of age.

Difficulty with joint attention, pretend play, communication, and repetitive behaviors have been suggested to be due to deficit executive function skills (Hughes 2001). Research has begun to hypothesize that delays in prefrontal cortical development play some role in the development of autism, due to the significant executive function deficits characteristic of the disorder. Debate continues among professionals as to whether executive function deficits in autism are a developmental difference or a delay. Experts also continue to hypothesize whether the executive function deficits are a related symptom or an underlying cause of autism. Nonetheless, an overview of the deficit executive function skills identified in children with autism is an interesting aspect of understanding the disorder.

Impaired executive function components associated with autism include the following characteristics:

- Inability to engage in goal-directed behavior
- Inability to adjust behavior to meet environmental demands
- Inability to perform multiple tasks simultaneously
- Inability to spontaneously adapt to changes in task requirements
- Inability to demonstrate flexible attention
- Difficulty with task planning
- Perseverative errors in task execution

In addition, children with high functioning autism may tend to demonstrate particular impairments in cognitive flexibility, planning, inhibiting responses, and verbal fluency.

Co-Morbidity of Executive Functions with Other Disorders

The ability to quickly shift the focus of planned, intentional behavior in response to changes in the environment is critical to goal-oriented, externally-driven outcomes. This cognitive flexibility is an important aspect of appropriate executive function. The perseverative, stereotypic behaviors typically seen in children with autism are standard-issue executive function deficits. The repetitive, non-goal-oriented behaviors of autism result in an inability to plan and perform tasks. Consequently, another person must provide external physical and verbal cues to prompt sequential and purposeful actions from the child with autism.

Some theories of executive function deficits in autism also suggest the possibility that the impaired development of social-emotional skills may be related to this inability to quickly adapt and shift attentional focus from one environmental stimulus to another. A typical development of the limbic system, which links to the orbitofrontal cortex of the prefrontal cortex and drives emotional impulses before they become modulated, is also suggested as a possible link to the early social impairments manifested in autism. This results in the extreme behavioral reactions to environmental stimuli so often seen in autism. The child's neurological system is not developed to modulate his reaction. In addition, the perseverative nature of the disorder (also characteristic of executive function deficits) results in the child maintaining the aberrant, non-purposeful response in a repetitive motor pattern.

Autism is a spectrum disorder with many possible types and causes speculated. As research begins to differentiate types of autism, the particular characteristic profiles may also refine. However, the development of executive function skills is always impaired to some degree and must be incorporated into treatment objectives.

Asperger's Syndrome/Nonverbal Learning Disorder and Executive Functions

Asperger's syndrome is included under autistic spectrum disorders but is a separate and distinct clinical entity. Diagnostic criterion for Asperger's syndrome includes significant impairment in reciprocal social communication and restricted, repetitive, stereotypic patterns of behavior in the presence of relatively appropriate language, intelligence, and adaptive behavior. Experts sometimes refer to Asperger's as the "genius syndrome" because the individuals tend to demonstrate a very astute mechanical aptitude for science, engineering, and math, with extreme deficits in reading and responding to social-emotional information. This discrepancy accounts for the social, emotional, and occupation problems characteristic of Asperger's syndrome.

Co-Morbidity of Executive Functions with Other Disorders

Nonverbal learning disorder is defined as a right hemisphere problem that results in difficulty understanding nonverbal information, including organization, evaluation, and holistic processing. Three areas of dysfunction are usually observed:

- Motor
- Visual-spatial
- Social

Children with nonverbal learning disorder appear "normal" in posture and appearance, as opposed to individuals with Asperger's syndrome who often stand out in a crowd by their peculiar motor movements and interaction style. The apparent masking of obvious deficits results in unrealistic demands and overestimates of a child's capability. The inaccurate interpretations of information around them causes children with nonverbal learning disorders to be perceived as behavior problems rather than acknowledging their legitimate learning deficits.

Impaired executive function components associated with Asperger's syndrome and nonverbal learning disorder include the following:

- Rigid thinking with focus on detail
- Poor understanding and recognition of nonverbal cues, such as facial expression, gesture, and vocal inflection
- Over-reliance on talk and poor inhibition for verbalization
- Difficulty generalizing rote learning to functional learning; difficulty interrelating information
- Poor motor planning and general disorganization
- Difficulty adapting to change; confused by complexity and novelty
- Poor problem solving and reasoning
- Difficulty with abstract conceptualization
- Poor self-regulation
- Impaired social interactions

Asperger's syndrome and nonverbal learning disorder are not the same disorder; however, the challenges in the area of executive functions are similar. Daniel Rosenn, M.D. (2001) discusses Asperger's and nonverbal learning disabilities as clinically overlapping disorders.

Research supports that premise, suggesting that as many as 80 percent of the individuals with Asperger's syndrome will also evidence a nonverbal learning disorder. Both disorders are due to neurological differences in the prefrontal and frontal lobe areas of the brain.

Co-Morbidity of Executive Functions with Other Disorders

There are several factors that relate Asperger's syndrome and nonverbal learning disorders. Research examining the originating cause of autism and related disorders is focusing on the fibers that link the cerebellum, basal ganglia, and prefrontal lobes. The corpus callosum, which connects the two cerebral hemispheres, is also thought to be involved. These structures are intensely involved in inhibitory control over thoughts, attention, and action. The relationship between working memory and inhibition may be the key to self-regulation, which is deficit in children with Asperger's syndrome and nonverbal learning disorder. The child doesn't know what to inhibit as irrelevant and what to retain as relevant within his mind. It becomes very difficult for the child to interrelate information from various areas of the brain, which is exactly the role of executive functions. Research by Casanova and associates (2002) indicates neurological and structural differences in children with these disorders. The result is too much communication, too little inhibition, and a tendency to shut out the rest of the world.

Children with Asperger's syndrome and nonverbal learning disorders have normal intellectual potential that is minimized by their difficulties in accurately reading subtle social-emotional cues. Deficits in executive function skills are a primary source of the limitations that occur in academic and social areas. Development of executive function skills will be the main focus of treatment goals for intervention to effectively allow these individuals to reach their intellectual potential.

Attention Deficit/Hyperactivity Disorder (ADD/ADHD) and Executive Functions

ADD/ADHD is a condition characterized by poor attention and impulse control, which can also be accompanied by hyperactivity. The features are evidenced during the developmental period before seven years of age. The inattention and impulsivity are displayed consistently in more than one setting and over a period of at least six months. The difficulty with sustaining attention typically leads to learning problems, which subsequently results in poor social skills, low self-esteem, and behavior problems.

The medical diagnostic criteria for ADD/ADHD is delineated in *The Diagnostic and Statistical Manual of Mental Disorders, Fourth Edition* (2000). Specific characteristics within categories of inattention, hyperactivity, and impulsivity are listed. In reviewing the list, many of the characteristic symptoms are clearly executive function skills.

Co-Morbidity of Executive Functions with Other Disorders

The impaired executive function components associated with ADD/ADHD include the following:

- Failure to attend to details, resulting in careless mistakes
- Difficulty sustaining attention to task
- Inability to follow through on instructions or finish tasks
- Difficulty organizing tasks and activities
- Easily distracted by extraneous stimuli
- Forgetful in daily activities
- Impulsive in verbal and motor responses
- Poor regulation of social behavior

The array of deficit executive function skills in ADD/ADHD are very different from the cognitive inflexibility impairments seen in autism. Many of the characteristics of ADD/ADHD are consistent with metacognitive disorders, which impact monitoring the major functions of the prefrontal cortex and executive function systems. Rather than a lack of engagement or awareness of environmental stimuli, children with ADD/ADHD are cognitively aware but unable to modulate their social-emotional behavioral responses. Acquired brain damage to the orbitofrontal cortex often produces symptoms similar to those seen in children with ADD/ADHD, including inattention, impulsive behavior and speech, poorly regulated emotions and social behavior, and generally disorganized goal-directed efforts (Ylvisaker & DeBonis 2000).

ADD/ADHD is considered a lifelong disorder, affecting not only children, but persisting into adolescence and adulthood. The executive function deficits resulting from poor attention and impulsivity lead to a multitude of social-emotional problems, particularly in the school setting.

Individuals with ADD/ADHD demonstrate high drop-out rates, expulsion, grade failure, and suspension during their academic careers. Many also meet the criteria for oppositional defiant or conduct disorders, as well as various emotional disorders, such as anxiety and depression.

Professionals also discuss whether the underlying executive function deficits can account for the etiology of ADD/ADHD versus being a secondary symptomatic characteristic. Current studies are exploring this question as well as others in relation to it. For example, research is attempting to determine if different patterns of executive function deficits are evidenced in ADD versus ADHD. When ADD/ADHD occurs with other disorders, such as learning disability or language impairment, does that change the profile of executive function

Co-Morbidity of Executive Functions with Other Disorders

deficits? The answers to these questions aren't available yet. However, the importance of addressing deficits in the development of executive function skills will definitely impact the long-term prognosis for success for individuals with ADD/ADHD.

Fetal Alcohol Syndrome (FAS) and Executive Functions

FAS is a group of physical and behavioral features that result from maternal consumption of alcohol during pregnancy. Alcohol has a strong toxic effect on a developing fetus. The resulting impact on an individual child will depend on the timing and duration of the alcohol consumption by the mother. The diagnosis of FAS is defined by the following three criteria:

- Prenatal and postnatal growth retardation
- Central nervous system dysfunction
- Craniofacial abnormalities

If a child doesn't present with all three categories of the diagnostic criteria, then fetal alcohol effect (FAE) is noted.

Children with FAS are often clinically described as presenting the same problems as individuals with acquired frontal lobe deficits. Research is beginning to neurologically substantiate that clinical finding. Prenatal ultrasound evaluations conducted on fetuses whose mothers exposed them to alcohol showed small frontal lobes, as compared to fetuses not exposed to alcohol in utero.

The impaired executive function components associated with FAS/FAE include the following:

- Difficulty changing strategies, especially when rules are uncertain
- Difficulty retaining important information in distracting situations
- Difficulty manipulating information in working memory
- Poor judgment, abstraction, and planning and problem-solving skills
- Poor impulse control
- Oppositional, stubborn, defiant behavior
- Lack of a sense of danger
- Poor at making transitions
- Inappropriate responses to social cues
- Poor understanding of consequences
- Poor attention
- Hyperactivity

Co-Morbidity of Executive Functions with Other Disorders

Significant emotional and behavioral problems are associated with FAS/FAE. Infants with FAS/FAE are often irritable and difficult to calm, resulting in consistent sustained crying. The irritability demonstrated as an infant develops into temper tantrums as the child moves into preschool age. Adaptive behavior scores are usually deficit in this group of children, even more than would be expected based on intelligence levels. The lack of responsiveness to rules and structure makes educational planning very difficult. The academic learning situation can be extremely challenging and frustrating.

The deficit executive function skills associated with FAS/FAE result in children experiencing significant difficulty when trying to function appropriately in everyday life. As adolescents, the problems can escalate into lying, stealing, and other behaviors associated with juvenile delinquency. As adults, these individuals continue to demonstrate poor adaptive skills for functioning. They have trouble keeping jobs, demonstrate poor judgment, and are unable to remain focused on tasks. Poor impulse control and decision-making skills interfere with successful social relationships.

Most of the executive function deficits that occur in children with FAS/FAE are a result of central nervous system abnormalities. An awareness of the significant challenges associated with FAS/FAE can be advantageous for the professional working with these children. Targeting deficit executive function skills early in educational intervention may prevent some of the escalation of behavioral and emotional problems that typically occurs later in life.

Tourette's Syndrome and Executive Functions

Tourette's syndrome is characterized by multiple involuntary motor and vocal tics. The symptoms can fluctuate, particularly during the onset and early developmental years of the disorder. The erratic course of development during childhood complicates accurate diagnosis, which can result in secondary emotional and behavior problems when an explanation for the unsettling features is lacking.

Research on Tourette's syndrome indicates that it is an inherited, neuropsychiatric movement disorder, characterized by chronic fluctuating tic behaviors. At onset during childhood through adolescence, the tics are classified as simple—sudden, brief, and meaningless. As the disorder progresses, tics become complex—slower, longer, and more purposeful. Examples of simple vocal tics include grunting, throat clearing, and barking. They progress to complex vocal tics, such as coprolalia (obscenities), echolalia

Co-Morbidity of Executive Functions with Other Disorders

(repeating something heard), and palilalia (repeating yourself). Simple motor tics can include head jerks, eye blinks, and shrugging the shoulders. Examples of complex motor tics include echokinesis (imitating movements of others) and sequenced gesture patterns. The neurobehavioral components are the most debilitating feature of the disorder, but other characteristics can minimize the ability to function effectively in everyday life.

The impaired executive function components associated with Tourette's syndrome include the following:

- Poor attention
- Impulsivity
- Distractibility
- Inflexibility and/or obsessive-compulsive tendencies

Neurological case studies have reported frontal lobe involvement in Tourette's syndrome. Gedye (1991) hypothesized that the etiology of Tourette's syndrome was based primarily on a frontal lobe dysfunction, specifically abnormal discharges in the medial basal region. This area is responsible for mediating involuntary motor tics. Gedye's premise was that the duration and recurrent nature of movements evidenced in Tourette's syndrome are similar to the duration and recurrent nature of involuntary movements observed during frontal lobe seizures.

Frontal lobe seizures often originate in the medial-prefrontal and cingulate cortex areas. Seizures mediated in the frontal lobe cause vagal nerve stimulation which is manifested in respiratory changes and the vocal production muscles that control the larynx and articulators. This results in grunts, gasps, and barks that are also observed in Tourette's syndrome. When medical practitioners explored etiologies known to cause frontal lobe seizures, they reported similar etiologies to be co-occurring in individuals with Tourette's. These etiologies correspond to specific and distinct areas of the frontal lobe, resulting in a variety of characteristics that can occur in Tourette's syndrome.

The combination of executive function deficits listed above often results in learning disabilities or splintered academic performance for individuals with Tourette's syndrome. Certainly the visible and audible tics associated with the disorder can lead to significant social, emotional, and vocational problems. The primary treatment for Tourette's syndrome is pharmacological; however many of the medications result in side effects that magnify some of the executive function deficits. Treatment goals should definitely include strategies to compensate for the challenges in executive function skills.

Co-Morbidity of Executive Functions with Other Disorders

Williams Syndrome and Executive Functions

Williams syndrome is a neurobehavioral congenital disorder with significant medical and developmental problems. Medical aspects of the disorder can include organ deficits in heart, kidney, and circulatory structures; visual problems include strabismus and hyperopia, as well as visual perceptual deficits; dental abnormalities include small, widely spaced teeth with a wide mouth and full lips; physical features include a small upturned nose, puffy eyes, and general small stature. A degree of cognitive deficit is also usually part of Williams syndrome, resulting in challenges for educational planning.

Individuals with Williams syndrome present a very different and fascinating configuration of executive function problems. These children and adults tend to be excessively social, outgoing, and eager to please. They enjoy verbal interaction and are unafraid of strangers, resulting in what is commonly called "cocktail party speech," an over-talkative incessant chatter about inconsequential things. An additional strength noted is an aptitude for music, characterized by perfect pitch. However, hyperacusis (enhanced hearing sensitivity) can lead to extreme annoyance for environmental noise, resulting in aberrant behaviors.

The impaired executive function components associated with Williams syndrome include the following:

- Hyperactivity
- Inattention to relevant stimuli
- Distractibility and impulsivity in both behaviors and verbalizations
- Difficulty moderating emotional impulses into appropriate responses
- Reduced flexibility and adaptability, resulting in apprehension regarding change
- Poor inhibition of verbalizations
- Difficulty initiating relevant responses to environment
- Reduced ability to develop strategies for simple, functional problems
- Poor planning, sequencing, and organization of problem-solving efforts

The majority (95%) of Williams syndrome cases are missing genetic material on chromosome 7. The remaining cases (5%) have the sequence of genes present, but they are inverted. The area of chromosome 7 that is compromised includes a sequence of 20 genes that includes a section responsible for the elastin protein, which provides strength and elasticity to vessel walls. This results in the "elfin" physical features associated with Williams syndrome, as well as the heart and blood vessel problems.

Co-Morbidity of Executive Functions with Other Disorders

The friendly, outgoing, expressive language observed in individuals with Williams syndrome can be deceiving. Professionals are often surprised by the polite, courteous interaction style when first encountering a child with the disorder. However, the superficial language quickly becomes problematic once the executive function deficits become apparent. For example, the child's inability to discriminate appropriate versus inappropriate topics for conversation in a public setting can be disconcerting to the casual conversational partner. The poor impulse control, limited attention, and lack of inhibition for verbal language can be challenging to address.

In addition, some children with Williams syndrome demonstrate deficit problem-solving skills, characterized by poor decision making, reduced ability to identify or generate relevant strategies for solving day-to-day problems, and poor organizational planning and sequencing. When faced with tasks that seem simple, the child may shut down entirely, demonstrating an inability to generate or initiate the first steps. Teachers and parents may find themselves frustrated as they "cue" by asking the child to sort the laundry or finish their homework. Although it seems obvious and simple, such a task may overwhelm the executive function system with a flood of incoming information that the child with Williams syndrome is not able to organize or sort. Without a plan, the child has a tendency to disengage in order to prevent over-stimulation.

The profile of executive function deficits may look similar to the list generated for other disorders, but the actual presentation in everyday life is very different. While children with William syndrome are engaging and enthusiastic individuals, the challenge to resolve deficits in the development of executive function skills are very real and compounded by the cognitive deficits associated with the disorder.

Fragile X Syndrome and Executive Functions

Fragile X is a genetic syndrome associated with mental retardation. Distinctive facial features include a narrow, elongated face with a prominent jaw and large, long ears. The forehead is very prominent and the eyelids droop. The oral cavity tends to have a high, arched palate and there is a risk of cleft palate as a component of the syndrome.

Co-Morbidity of Executive Functions with Other Disorders

Communication and behavior issues are compounded by the cognitive deficits inherent within Fragile X. Learning issues, as well as management problems in the home and educational setting, can be challenging. In addition, a percentage of children (approximately 10%) within the Fragile X profile are also diagnosed with autism. As discussed earlier in this chapter, the autistic spectrum presents significant problems in the area of developing executive function skills.

The impaired executive function components associated with Fragile X Syndrome include the following:

- Hyperactivity
- Impulsivity
- Inattention, or shortened attention span
- Tendencies toward perseverative behaviors
- Poor sequencing and organization
- Poor perception of social cues
- Poor emotional regulation, resulting in impulsive bursts of expression (tantrums)
- Associated discipline problems, as a result of deficits listed above

Fragile X is a hereditary disorder in which a fragile portion on the long arm of the X chromosome causes the tip to become narrowed. It is second only to Down syndrome as a genetic cause of mental retardation. The physical facial features are usually accompanied by a series of other medical components. Hypotonicity and joint problems lead to poor coordination. Visual problems can include strabismus, nystagmus, and farsightedness.

The syndrome occurs less frequently in females, and characteristics tend to be milder. As a result, female children with Fragile X may develop higher levels of learning and language abilities, but then experience difficulties in abstraction, tangential language, and poor narrative skills due to the executive function deficits. Each child within Fragile X will present a unique profile that must be carefully analyzed by professionals involved in generating intervention goals.

Co-Morbidity of Executive Functions with Other Disorders

Childhood Traumatic Brain Injury and Executive Functions

The focus of this book is on development of executive function skills. Children who experience significant head trauma or brain injury during childhood would technically be diagnosed as having an acquired problem. However, depending on the age of insult, the developmental process of refining executive function skills with increased age would be impacted. At the point that the next expected level should develop, the deficit as a result of the injury would become apparent. Consequently, continued age-appropriate development of executive function skills could be compromised.

At the age of the actual brain injury or trauma, the demand for more complex executive function skills may not be apparent or needed, and therefore not assessed or observed. As early adolescence approaches, parents or professionals may begin to notice that the child is not able to perform as expected, and may be viewed as impulsive with poor self-control and attention when compared to same age peers. In general, the younger a child, the better chance for a good recovery. However, professionals need to be aware of the head trauma and monitor the expected executive function developmental levels. If the expected neuromaturational processes do not occur, intervention should be initiated.

Intervention needs to be based on the profile of executive function strengths and weaknesses apparent at the time they are observed. What may have been considered a relative strength at an earlier age, may become a weakness as the child grows. As expectations increase, normal developmental changes fail to occur. In fact, some children may not be diagnosed with deficit executive function skills immediately following an acquired brain injury. More obvious impairments may be identified only after the next expected level of development does not occur. "She acts just like a 17-year-old, except she's 24." This is a direct quote from the parents of a young woman who sustained two closed head injuries in her mid- to late teens and whose early recovery went relatively well. However, final maturation of the prefrontal cortex and executive function skills failed to take place; the young woman's ensuing life choices and ability to establish goals, plan for, and initiate action toward those life goals were impaired. This is an all too familiar and tragic example of the long-term results of the impact that an acquired brain injury has on the normal developmental process for executive functions.

Co-Morbidity of Executive Functions with Other Disorders

Summary

Many students with problems in development of adequate executive function skills are misdiagnosed with labels such as oppositional defiant disorder, conduct disorder, or emotional/behavior disorder. Significant problems in executive functions certainly put children at risk for vocational, social, and legal problems. If a composite list of the primary aspects of deficits across all the disorders discussed in this chapter were compiled, it could include the following:

- Poorly controlled behavior
- Poor choice-making skills
- Impulsive and inattentive actions
- Failure to adapt to surroundings
- Inability to organize or initiate goal-directed behavior
- Poor self-awareness and regulation

This list of behaviors will contribute to poor academic performance and eventual loss of work opportunities. The long-term ramifications are dependent on social safety nets and families. Hanging out with the "wrong" crowd can lead to juvenile delinquency or criminal charges that cause the individual to end up in the penal system.

Accurate, early diagnosis of deficits within the context of other childhood disorders is key. The intervention objectives need to address primary deficits but must encompass specific and direct treatment to manage executive function deficits. By teaching students how to self-regulate and learn behaviors and communication skills that are socially and vocationally appropriate, the chances for their future success and independence are enhanced.

Effective speech-language treatment has evolved toward being proactive in reducing risk of future problems by better understanding the total impact of developmental disorders. An intervention program that includes objectives to address executive function skills will force professionals to think more about treating the whole child, not just an isolated language or communication problem. Treatment for any communication disorder should include consideration of how to facilitate better executive function skills. Communication goals should teach a child to be flexible and adaptive to other people and the environment. Self-awareness and self-control are critical aspects of both verbal and nonverbal effectiveness.

Co-Morbidity of Executive Functions with Other Disorders

If isolated areas of speech-language deficits become the whole focus, then the therapist is prone to lose the reason for working so hard to develop communication skills. Development of executive function skills should be a product of speech-language therapy. It should drive the **what** and **why** of therapy with a child whose communication is not well-regulated by metacognition.

The professionals who work with children who have disorders cannot underestimate the impact of executive function skills. A child needs to be able to gather additional information from observing a person's face, body language, vocal intonation, and prosody. Modifications in what a child does and says are prompted and governed by reflecting on the meaning within those observations. The individual who cannot "read" beyond the actual words spoken will be minimally successful in various life pursuits.

As the professionals charged with remediating communication disorders, we can do a better job of treating these issues. An intelligent little boy with Asperger's syndrome, who cannot take the perspective of others, who cannot control his impulsive anger, who is inflexible unless the environment meets his own quirky interests, who cannot read facial expressions or identify how his words and actions may impact someone else, is not going to ever realize his potential unless someone directly addresses the deficits and develops the ability to "put it all together." That's what executive function skills are!

> As speech-language pathologists, we need to think about these concepts each time we encounter a child with ADD/ADHD or fetal alcohol syndrome. How are we going to help the child achieve his goals in life? Communication cannot be separated from the person and the environment. It must be adaptive and reflective so a child can share internal ideas with external constituents. We have an obligation to teach the child vocabulary, concepts, and processing skills. To do this job well, we must use those foundation skills to bridge into metacognitive aspects of communication encompassed with executive function skills.

The Source for Development of Executive Functions
Copyright © 2005 LinguiSystems, Inc.

Chapter 4
Assessment of Executive Functions

Overview

Speech-language pathologists are accustomed to using assessment tools that examine very specific pieces of knowledge, rather than how the child uses and manages that knowledge. A professional giving a test acts in a manner very similar to the prefrontal cortex, by keeping the child's attention focused, eliminating external distractions, monitoring task completion within given time constraints, etc. Test administration rules also tend to eliminate any possibility for error in individual planning or sequencing because the responses are simply given and recorded. Individual goal selection is eliminated from the testing process as tasks are carefully controlled and examiner ordered.

> The main difference in evaluating executive function skills is that the examiner must be careful not to build herself in as the child's prefrontal cortex, so that the child can independently demonstrate her executive function skills.

One of the main hallmarks of standardized testing is the fact that the examiner must follow scripted administration procedures, adhering to the rules and requirements of identified test parameters. Evaluating the capacity of a child to use and apply knowledge via the prefrontal cortex in order to determine the presence of executive function impairment requires a whole different approach to testing.

In fact, assessment of executive function skills is problematic on a number of levels, only one of which is the examiner acting as a surrogate prefrontal cortex.

Executive Function Assessment Principles

▶ Deficits in fundamental language skills

One complication is the fact that executive function skills are a result of tertiary processing. Executive function skills are integrative, and therefore dependent upon the quality of incoming information from primary and secondary processing areas. If deficits exist in the processing of incoming information, the quality of meaning attached to incoming stimuli and sent to the prefrontal cortex for executive function management will automatically impact the quality of decision making. Accurate assessment of executive function skills will indirectly reflect how intact or impaired a child's general language and processing skills are. Impairment in any of these lower-order, prerequisite skills may result in a poor overall score in the absence

Assessment of Executive Functions

of true executive function deficits. Think back to the orchestra analogy presented on pages 8-9. The deficit could be with the conductor, musicians, or both. It requires a skilled examiner to tease through the different possible combinations of deficits and to distinguish between executive function deficits and other impairments.

▶ **Strengths and weaknesses**

It is also important to understand that careful assessment of executive function skills needs to distinguish between components a child has difficulty with and those that are strengths. An evaluation of executive function skills should compile a profile of strengths and weaknesses so that intervention can be effectively designed. It is entirely possible that a child will have some well-developed executive function skills, while others are delayed or atypical in their development.

For example, a child may have excellent attention and be able to focus on a complex task in the presence of highly distracting and competing stimuli. But if the child is unable to generate a goal-driven strategy or organize materials and plans, then excellent attention by itself will not result in successful completion of the task. On the other hand, a child may be skilled in strategies and planning but demonstrate poorly controlled impulsivity that causes her to jump erratically from one part of the task to the next. Some children may even be able to verbalize what they should do (from a metacognitive perspective) but be unable to either initiate or carry out those plans. Some children can identify a plan, read nonverbal social cues, and organize their thoughts and information, yet are unable to initiate work on the task or interaction. These children often appear to be "stuck" and require different kinds of intervention than those who are constantly active and need to slow down. An effective evaluation should identify the child's profile of executive function skill development in order to build on strengths and compensate for or teach strategies for weaker skills.

▶ **Specific executive function skills**

Another critical concept to keep in mind is that tests that look at specific executive function skills are more useful than tests that only provide a global summary of problem-solving or social interaction skills. Executive function skills must be delineated rather than evaluated as a whole in order to correctly identify target areas for remediation. In order to design a relevant and effective treatment plan, assessment data must identify deficit skills as specifically as possible.

Assessment of Executive Functions

Impairments associated with deficits in executive function skills can affect social interaction and pragmatic communication, functional problem solving, the ability to learn and integrate new information, the capacity to remember information needed to successfully execute tasks and basic life skills, or the ability to use language as a means of self-regulation. These are just a few examples of the observed impact that results from executive function deficits. Depending on which cluster of executive function components are involved, a child may exhibit impairments primarily in social skills, in problem solving, or perhaps with memory.

The choice of testing materials is somewhat dependent on the types of difficulty a child is perceived to have. Some childhood disorders, such as Asperger's syndrome, present with the characteristic of social inflexibility, which impacts pragmatic social development. Conducting an evaluation would require the use of formal or informal measures designed to assess social pragmatic skills of reciprocal interaction, rather than attention or memory, which are usually strengths within the Asperger profile. Conversely, a child with a diagnosis of Williams syndrome might need an assessment based more on reasoning and problem solving than initiating social skills, which is generally strong.

▶ Developmental expectations

Consistent with assessment of any other developmental skill, the examiner must consider the developmental stage of a child and her mental cognitive capacity. Four-year-old children demonstrate very different executive function skills than fourteen-year-old adolescents. Expectations increase and change with maturation and experience. Sustained attention and working memory improve to the degree that an adolescent can begin to mentally manipulate more complex problems with multiple variables, as compared to the preschool child who can only handle one variable in a situation. An adolescent begins to develop the ability to generate goals, which reflects anticipation of more long-term consequences, although impulsivity may still interfere with the ability to successfully execute the plan. Problem-solving abilities are also very different in the adolescent who is beginning to incorporate strategic thinking and the ability to learn from failures. It is important to use developmental information to determine which executive functions skills are appropriate for various age levels so expectations are reasonable and accurate.

Assessment of Executive Functions

▶ Impact of intelligence level

In a child who possesses a high intelligence quotient, some executive function tests may not be sensitive enough to pick up on subtle deficits. In general, IQ tests look at what can be called crystallized intelligence, rather than performance or fluid intelligence. According to the Cattell-Horn-Cattell (CHC) theory of intellectual processing, *crystallized intelligence* refers to the use of acquired knowledge and learned skills in order to provide responses. Typically, tests of "set" knowledge observe verbal abilities, including general knowledge and vocabulary. The *Woodcock-Johnson III* (Woodcock, McGrew, & Mather 2001) includes a cluster of subtests that assesses crystallized knowledge called Comprehension-Knowledge (Verbal Comprehension, General Information).

In contrast to evaluation of acquired or learned verbal knowledge is assessment of how information is used to perform inductive and deductive reasoning for novel, unfamiliar tasks that require integrative thinking. The CHC theory refers to this type of intelligence as *fluid intelligence*, which on the *Woodcock-Johnson III* is reflected in a cluster of subtests known as Fluid Reasoning (Analysis-Synthesis, Concept Formation). Scores on these subtests reflect the capacity to plan strategic efforts, anticipate outcomes, monitor and correct performance, inhibit impulsive and ineffective responses, and develop and apply strategies to changing rules. They also account for the ability to form conclusions, draw upon working memory to learn from previous efforts, and divide complex attention across multiple factors. Observation of the process used by a child, as well as interpretation of these scores, provide excellent insight into executive function performance.

The distinction here is that evaluating IQ is not the same as evaluating executive functions. *Crystallized intelligence* is a stored body of acquired knowledge; *fluid intelligence* is the use and application of that knowledge to novel circumstances that require integration, metacognition, and adaptability. Tasks that assess fluid intelligence must be novel, unfamiliar, and require the individual to draw conclusions and inferences that have not previously been understood or learned. Integrative thinking, planning strategic efforts, anticipating outcomes, monitoring and correcting performance, and shifting attention to new rules are all definitions encompassed within executive function skills.

Assessment of Executive Functions

▶ **Process versus product**

The previous discussion highlights another critical point in understanding assessment of executive function skills. No matter which type of assessment is chosen, evaluating executive function components is primarily about looking at a process. The quality of the process must be determined; the individual components of the process for using knowledge must be profiled. How a child solves a problem, learns a new task, or regulates emotional/social behavior in ever-changing environments must be fluid and simultaneous. Adaptability is key; providing stock responses to novel circumstances is ineffective and likely to be unsuccessful. In the case of evaluating executive function skills, you don't necessarily want to tap into stored knowledge at all. What you want to do is tap into the child's capacity to use and apply this information.

> How a child works through novel and unpredictable situations is a more true measure of her capacity to determine an appropriate course of action, develop a strategy, sequence the steps required, monitor the execution of planned efforts to achieve a deliberate and successful outcome, initiate useful behaviors and inhibit impulsive or destructive behaviors, and modulate social behavior in accordance with expected social parameters.

Clinical therapy rooms are usually closed off to the outside world to provide a quiet, nondistracting environment. In most cases, this works well; but when evaluating executive function skills, the controlled environment could actually mask the presence of deficits by providing a structured setting and an examiner who plans and initiates most of the assessment tasks. The most useful evaluations of executive function skills often take place in the child's regular environment, such as in the classroom, at a playground, at home, or when interacting with other children. This requires the use of observational instruments and an understanding of what characteristics to look for as a child attempts to organize and manage the demands of the day.

Review of Assessment Instruments

Conversations and interviews with parents and teachers provide significant insight regarding the development of executive function skills. The examiner needs to gain an understanding of how a child is able to attend and remain on task, how often impulsive behavior is observed to interfere with assignments or chores, or how aware a child is of performing within the given rules and expectations of a teacher or parent.

Assessment of Executive Functions

Parents often describe behavior of a child with executive function deficits as being disorganized or scattered. Constant prompting and reminding is necessary. These children require very specific directions in order to accurately complete simple tasks.

> For example, a parent can't give a simple direction, such as "Please pick up your dirty laundry" and expect it to be completed accurately. Instead, the parent has to provide direction through all phases of the task, such as "Please pick up your dirty laundry, all of it; put it in the laundry basket; take it to the laundry room; check under the bed; look all over the floor; don't forget the socks over there; what about this shirt on the bed?"

Typical patterns emerge in parent and teacher interviews as they describe a child with deficits in executive function skills. Parents may describe a child who is constantly inattentive and impulsive, who gets into frequent behavioral trouble at school, or who is unable to be on time and carry out time-sensitive activities. Teachers may notice that a child can only complete a worksheet if given one-on-one assistance to plan out where to start and how to continue working until finished. Students with executive function deficits find it difficult to complete tasks they perceive as being overwhelming, even if the content is something they are familiar with.

There are very few standardized tests to evaluate the development of executive function skills, and those that exist still have some environment-test administrator issues to overcome. Formal tests in the area of executive functions are less readily available than language tests in the areas of vocabulary, concepts, syntax, pragmatics, etc. As a profession, speech-language pathology has focused on the evaluation and treatment of more discrete aspects of communication, rather than the integrative application of language skills inherent within executive functions. But as we increase our understanding of how communication, both behavioral and verbal, is affected by and linked to normal and atypical executive function development, we will see a corresponding growth of instruments designed to evaluate these skills. As such, there are an increasing number of formal, standardized tests and behavioral checklists becoming available for our use.

> Integrating impressions from informal observations with information obtained from parent–teacher interviews and any formal tools is the most effective approach for evaluating executive function skills.

The Source for Development of Executive Functions

Assessment of Executive Functions

While speech-language pathology has been somewhat slow to acknowledge executive function skills, the field of psychology has been evaluating frontal lobe skills for a number of years and has many excellent tests at its disposal. Table 4.1 summarizes many of the tools you might see referenced in a school psychologist's report or a neuropsychologist's consultation.

Table 4.1 Tests of Frontal Lobe Functioning Used in Psychology

Test	Skills Evaluated
NEPSY	Evaluates executive function skills in children, including auditory attention, planning, flexibility, impulsivity, self-monitoring and regulation, and problem solving
Porteus Mazes	Evaluates the process of planning, organizing, and predicting outcomes as subject attempts to navigate a complex maze without hitting a wall or dead end
Trail Making Test	Requires visual scanning and attention, processing speed, and cognitive flexibility for shifting and sequencing alternating number and letter patterns
Children's Color Trails Test (CCTT)	Assesses sustained attention, sequencing, and flexibility without demanding language skills Normed for ages 8-16
Tower of London DX (2nd ed.)	Highly sensitive to attention deficits noted in ADHD
Controlled Oral Word Association Test (COWAT)	Measures verbal fluency, which is highly sensitive to frontal lobe function
Wisconsin Card Sorting Test	Includes number of trials completed, number of correct responses, number and percentage of errors, number and percentage of perseverative responses, number and percentage of nonperseverative errors, number of categories correctly identified, number of trials to completion of the first category, number and percentage of conceptual level responses, number of set breaks (making an incorrect response after a run of six correct responses), and the "learning to learn" factor
Conners' Continuous Performance Test	Measures attention Observes response patterns that indicate inattentiveness, impulsivity, poor initiation, or inability to maintain vigilant, persistent attention

continued on next page

Assessment of Executive Functions

Table 4.1, continued Tests of Frontal Lobe Functioning Used in Psychology

Test	Skills Evaluated
Rey Complex Figure Test and Recognition Trial (RCFT)	Assesses visual spatial recall, recognition, construction, and processing speed
Stroop Color and Word Test	Measures mental flexibility and ability to inhibit responses to interfering stimuli in individuals ages 16-80
Stroop Color and Word Test: Children's Version	Assesses deficits in executive functions such as inhibition, planning, and impulsivity Normed for children ages 5-14
Ruff Figural Fluency Test	Evaluates fluid thinking, initiation, mental flexibility, planning, and divergent reasoning Normed for ages 16-70

Before selecting a battery of tests or observations, it is necessary to consider the child's needs, the diagnosis she may have, the descriptions of the child's difficulties by both parents and teachers, and your own observations of the child. At the heart of assessment is the need to determine why the child is experiencing the deficits observed. Designing an effective treatment plan is dependent upon knowing which executive function skills are in deficit in order to work from the inside out, so to speak.

For example, addressing social skills will be far more successful given an understanding of whether the issue is one of language impairments or is also compounded by inflexibility, inattention, poor self-regulation of impulsive drives, or an impaired capacity to take the perspective of others by reading nonverbal social cues. Treating deficits in problem solving will be far more successful if there is a clear delineation between impaired language processing, for example, and deficit executive function skills such as goal identification, planning and organization, initiation, adaptability, and self-correction. Other children with impaired self-help skills due to poor problem solving may require assistance using abstract reasoning to predict outcomes, to anticipate consequences of efforts, or to draw conclusions and infer the necessary materials to successfully complete a task. Working on verbal memory for instructions or explanations may be entirely dependent on laying a foundation of attention skills and organization of verbal information. Careful test selection should help a professional highlight areas of deficit to formulate a treatment plan.

The Source for Development of Executive Functions
Copyright © 2005 LinguiSystems, Inc.

Assessment of Executive Functions

There are a number of standardized tests that have been designed to evaluate the development of executive function skills in children and adolescents. The parameters discussed previously in this chapter must be considered when choosing the instruments to use. An instrument will only address what it has been designed to accomplish. The professional must always supplement and interpret, using her own clinical impressions and knowledge.

Table 4.2 provides a summary of standardized assessment tools. Information for each test includes the ages evaluated and some general comments of what the instrument is designed to evaluate. You may want to add formal tests of pragmatics, reasoning, and functional memory to your battery.

Table 4.2 Standardized Tests for Executive Functions—Children & Adolescents

Ages	Test	Comments
6-18	Behavioral Assessment of the Dysexecutive Syndrome in Children (BADS-C)	Evaluates flexibility, perseveration, novel problem solving, sequencing, use of feedback, planning, impulsivity, and following instructions
6-18	Dysexecutive Questionnaire (component of the BADS-C as above)	Identifies four areas of difficulty related to executive function deficits: emotional/personality issues, motivation, behavioral and cognitive difficulty
6-18	Test of Everyday Attention for Children (TEA-Ch)	Evaluates sustained attention Reaction time subtest requires the subject to name all digits appearing on a screen at a constant rate except for a particular digit that occurs randomly approximately every 1 out of 9 trials Children with ADHD perform poorly on this subtest due to impaired sustained attention to task.

continued on next page

Assessment of Executive Functions

Table 4.2, *continued* **Standardized Tests for Executive Functions—Children & Adolescents**

Ages	Test	Comments
9-59	d2 Test of Attention	Measures sustained attention, processing speed, motivation and task persistence, inhibitory control, rule compliance, quality and consistency of work over time
16-70	Ruff 2 & 7 Selective Attention Test	Measures sustained and selective visual attention, with 20 trials of search and cancellation tasks for two target digits that are either embedded among other numbers or alphabet letters
5-14	Stroop Color and Word Test–Children's Version	Assesses inhibition, suppression of irrelevant responses, perseveration, sustained attention, and flexibility in frontal lobe populations
9-14	Children's Trail Making Test A & B (a component of the Halstead-Reitan Neuropsychological Test Battery)	Measures subtle deficits in alternating and sustained attention, sequencing, shifting sets Used extensively as a screening device to identify altered neurological functioning in children, and is especially sensitive to children with ADHD
8-16	Children's Color Trails Test (also known as Kids Color Trails)	Measures subtle deficits in alternating and sustained attention, sequencing, and shifting sets Eliminates linguistically-loaded stimuli (letters) and relies on colors and numbers instead
Preschool-Adult	Woodcock-Johnson III (WJ III) Tests of Cognitive Abilities (Analysis-Synthesis, Concept Formation, Numbers Reversed subtests)	Individual subtests assess both intellectual and academic development, distinguishing between fluid and crystallized intelligence (Executive function skills more reflected in fluid reasoning subtests)

The Source for Development of Executive Functions

Assessment of Executive Functions

In addition to standardized evaluation instruments, there are also a few good behavioral rating scales for identifying strengths and weaknesses in executive function skills. These scales are summarized in Table 4.3 below.

Table 4.3 Behavioral Rating Scales for Executive Functions—Children and Adolescents

Ages	Test	Comments
2.0-5.11	Behavior Rating Inventory of Executive Function— Preschool (BRIEF-P)	Two different questionnaires, one for parents and one for teachers of preschool children Assesses five specific executive function skills in the home and preschool environments: inhibit, shift, emotional control, working memory, and plan/organize Provides three broader indexes: inhibitory self-control, flexibility, and emergent metacognition Provides an overall global executive composite score
5-18	Behavior Rating Inventory of Executive Function (BRIEF)	Two different questionnaires, one for parents and one for teachers of school-age children Eight clinical scales measure specific components of executive function: inhibit, shift emotional control, initiate, working memory, plan/organize, organization of materials, and monitor Frequency of problem behaviors is rated as *never*, *sometimes*, or *always* Provides two broader indexes: behavioral regulation and metacognition Provides a global score of executive function (global executive composite)
11-18	Behavior Rating Inventory of Executive Function— Self Report (BRIEF-SR)	Standardized self-report measure of executive function skills from the adolescent's own point of view, providing invaluable insight into self-awareness within the everyday environment Scales measure the following executive function components: inhibit, shift, emotional control, monitor, working memory, plan/organize, organization of materials, and task completion Two subscales, behavioral shift and cognitive shift, and two validity scales, inconsistency and negativity, are also derived from scores Global executive composite reflects an overall score

Assessment of Executive Functions

Informal Assessment of Executive Functions

Even though formal tests are becoming more widely available for assessment of executive function skills, they may not be included in the battery of tests at your disposal. This does not mean that you can't evaluate a child for the presence of impaired executive function abilities. Often, the most important aspect of assessment for executive function deficits is a skilled observation of the child in a classroom, on a playground, at home, or in therapy. Of course, you must know what you are looking for. Conversations with parents and teachers are also extremely helpful, regardless of whether you use a standardized behavioral checklist or simply visit with them informally.

> In therapy, one of the most useful ways to evaluate executive function skills is to establish conditions that require the child to develop and execute plans, regulate her performance and attention, and use language to help her meet normal environmental or social expectations.

Many of the case examples highlighted in this chapter on pages 100-115 reflect a combination of extensive informal assessment and formal tests results. Preparing for informal assessment of executive function skills requires some initial planning, particularly in designing functional activities to observe the child apply cognitive and linguistic processing skills to demands within various functional tasks. It also requires a shift in thinking from being the "director" of a diagnostic session to being more of an uninvolved bystander. This is somewhat counter-intuitive to the way of thinking for most traditional evaluations and can be the most challenging part of the assessment. We cue our clients almost without thinking during therapy, providing just enough of a boost to help them achieve the desired production. But in a good assessment of executive function skills, cueing only serves to mask potential deficits by making up for the child's inability to self-direct.

There are a variety of components that may be included in an informal assessment of executive function skills. Depending on the needs of the child, concerns expressed by the parent or teacher, and the overall goals of the child and family, you may include all or some of the following:

- Interviews and conversations—parent, teacher, child
- Observation of problem-solving skills—functional tasks for life skills, novel tasks
- Observation of social interaction—academic performance/classroom behavior, social interaction with peers

The Source for Development of Executive Functions
Copyright © 2005 LinguiSystems, Inc.

Assessment of Executive Functions

Each of these components is explored and exemplified in the sections below. Sample tasks and skills to assess are included, as well as characteristics or behaviors to look for as you evaluate the child's executive function skills.

▶ Interviews and conversations

Undoubtedly, the easiest and quickest way to begin preparing an interview for caregivers is to use the standardized behavioral checklists and rating scales referenced on pages 74-76. These tools include the *Dysexecutive Questionnaire* component of the *BADS-C* for children 6-18 and the *BRIEF* questionnaires for parents and teachers of children from preschool through 18 years of age. Collectively, these questionnaires help identify behaviors seen in the home and school that are typical of children with executive function deficits. The *BRIEF-SR*, as noted previously, is an excellent tool for assessing the perceptions and awareness of adolescents. A discrepancy will often be noted between the observations of a child and of those with whom she interacts on a daily basis. Identifying this difference in perceptions is a key component to successful development of a treatment plan. If a child lacks awareness, then all the effort in the world will not result in the child independently implementing any newly learned skill or compensatory strategy.

In general, looking for a profile of strengths and weaknesses is useful once you have insight into how the child uses executive function skills in her environment. As with any other diagnostic conversation, you want to adapt your questions as the informant presents different examples and characterizations of the child. You may choose to expand your line of questioning significantly into one particular aspect of executive function skills, or you may stay with a broad perspective. When thinking about the kinds of questions to ask a parent or teacher, consider also asking how often these behaviors are observed, to what degree they interfere with the child's ability to function independently, and how often and what kind of cues are needed.

The questions are not designed to single out the typically-developing child who acts like a four-year-old because he *is* a four-year-old. Rather, they are designed to be used by a skilled interpreter who is aware of normal developmental profiles and expectations. Many of the children who may be referred for assessment of executive function skills may have histories of behavior problems, aggression, constant need for one-on-one help to complete simple tasks, or have parents who are at a loss for how to assist their child. Deficits in executive function skills may not be identified in a child until later stages of development when same-aged peers move on to

Assessment of Executive Functions

more advanced stages of self-help or problem solving, and the difficulties become more apparent.

Parent Interview. Typically, parents of these children are very willing to talk with an interested listener. It is common for parents to demonstrate exasperation at their child's behavior but also express guilt for feeling frustrated. "She makes me want to pull my hair out" may be a common response followed by "Isn't that awful?" Or the parents' frustration may be even more significant, including expressed fear over their adolescent child's aggressive behavior. "I'm afraid to be at home alone with him" is not an uncommon statement, although it may take a long time before a parent is willing to admit to feeling this kind of fear. Many parents find themselves increasingly worried about their child's poor organizational thinking and self-monitoring skills as the school year ends and plans for the coming year are being put into place. "How will she be able to cope? Who will help her? What if she gets kicked out?" These are the kinds of responses you can expect to hear during conversations with parents.

Teacher Interview. Teachers also tend to see children with deficit executive function skills as needing a considerable amount of extra time and help. These students take a lot of energy from classroom instructors, whether it is the primary teacher, a classroom assistant, or an aide. In IEP meetings, listen for teacher descriptions that include comments like "needs help getting started, needs to be told exactly what to do, needs constant reminders to stay on task, is easily overwhelmed or frustrated, is unable to interact well with others, cannot transition easily," or "needs lots of notice to get ready to switch tasks." Other descriptions of children with executive function deficits might not be expressed so tactfully, such as "lazy, forgetful, doesn't try, distracts the class, takes up all my time, just won't work, doesn't pay attention, doesn't listen," or "just needs to learn." Children with executive function deficits can be very trying for a teacher on a day-to-day basis.

Child Interview. Finally, conversations with the child may prove to be the most insightful. You will often have had discussions with the parent, caregiver, or teacher before encountering the child in a diagnostic situation. At that point, it is useful to select questions that reflect the trends noted from previous conversations with adults in the child's life. The purpose of a conversation with the child is to determine the extent of the child's awareness of her weaknesses. Self-awareness is not an automatic skill; it is part of metacognition, which regulates the self for planning, anticipating, focusing, adapting, and correcting. If a child has trouble recognizing deficits in executive function components, it is likely that she is unable to perceive

The Source for Development of Executive Functions
Copyright © 2005 LinguiSystems, Inc.

Assessment of Executive Functions

the effect her words or actions have on others, and she will be unable to correct or modify her behaviors. The result is a child who presents a little bit like someone who sees the world through rose-colored glasses. She believes all is well and problems don't bother her.

Sample Questions. The following sample questions outline some good starting points for these conversations. The lists are not intended for you to ask all of the questions. Instead, they are designed to provide a guideline in generating the types of questions to pursue with parents, teachers, or children suspected of having executive function deficits.

A. Sample Interview Questions for Parent or Caregiver

1. What can your child do well at home?
2. What tasks does your child need help with at home that you would expect him/her to be able to do?
3. Why do you think your child has difficulty with these tasks, whether they are self-help or chore-related?
4. How often have you explained or shown your child how to do these tasks?
5. What kinds of cues or reminders does your child depend on each day?
6. Does your child have trouble concentrating on tasks?
7. How long can your child attend to an activity before losing his/her train of thought or forgetting what he/she was doing?
8. Does your child have difficulty completing tasks or organizing his/her approach to a chore?
9. Can your child complete his/her homework without one-on-one direction?
10. Does your child lose his/her place in homework, conversations, projects, or other tasks?
11. Does your child need specific direction to get started?
12. Can your child plan out what he/she needs to accomplish a task?

continued on next page

Assessment of Executive Functions

13. Does your child become upset easily by unexpected changes in his/her routine?

14. Is your child impulsive in his/her actions or thoughts?

15. Does your child often act before thinking or perform things in an unsafe manner?

16. Is your child aware of how his/her actions impact others?

17. Can your child solve problems or come up with alternative plans if the first ones are unsuccessful?

18. Is your child restless?

19. Does your child often say things that are not age-appropriate in social situations?

20. Does your child seem to be able to understand others' feelings and needs?

21. Can your child get ready for the day without unnecessary distractions, interruptions, forgetfulness, or disorganization?

22. Does your child often interrupt others?

23. Does your child often get into fights or disagreements with others?

24. How well does your child control anger or frustration?

25. Does your child say or do the same things over and over?

26. Can your child finish tasks once they are started?

27. Does your child miss obvious details or parts of a task?

28. Does your child lose things, such as lunch money, papers, and shoes?

29. Can your child manage simple self-help tasks independently?

30. Can your child plan ahead for activities and anticipate when he/she needs to get ready?

31. Can your child predict how well or poorly he/she will complete work?

32. Is your child aware of being offensive, inattentive, disorganized, or forgetful?

continued on next page

The Source for Development of Executive Functions
Copyright © 2005 LinguiSystems, Inc.

Assessment of Executive Functions

B. Sample Interview Questions for Teacher

1. Does the student lose his/her train of thought?
2. Can the student pay attention to class instructions without becoming distracted?
3. Does the student forget what he/she was doing?
4. Can the student complete assignments without forgetting the instructions or losing his/her place?
5. Does the student have an organized backpack and desk?
6. How well can the student organize projects or end-of-the-day work to take home?
7. How often does the student need one-on-one help to stay focused on an assignment that others complete independently?
8. Does the child check his/her work for mistakes?
9. Can the child fix his/her mistakes?
10. Is the child able to find his/her way around school after a reasonable amount of time?
11. How well does the child interact with peers and teachers?
12. Does the child demonstrate socially appropriate behaviors?
13. Can the child switch from task to task according to the day's schedule?
14. Can the child handle unexpected changes in the day?
15. Does the student often act without thinking or planning?
16. Does the student have difficulty planning ahead for an activity?
17. How well can the student complete assignments, once started?
18. Is the child aware of the consequences of his/her words and actions?
19. Does the student demonstrate incomplete or careless work?
20. How well can the student control his/her behavior?

continued on next page

Assessment of Executive Functions

21. How much specific direction does the child need to complete familiar activities?

22. How well can the child complete unfamiliar tasks?

23. Can the student develop plans and strategies?

C. Sample Interview Questions for Child

1. Do you ever have difficulty staying focused on your work or activities?
2. Do you feel that you become distracted easily?
3. How well are you able to organize your work, chores, or other activities?
4. Do you have a messy backpack, room, or desk?
5. Can you find things that you need?
6. Can you easily finish a project once you have started it?
7. Are you able to control feelings of anger or frustration?
8. Do you feel that you are impulsive?
9. Do you make careless mistakes?
10. Are you forgetful?
11. Does it take you longer than others to complete your work?
12. Do you need help organizing projects or chores?
13. Do you adjust well to unexpected changes?
14. Do you solve problems easily?
15. Do you anticipate consequences of your actions?
16. Do you double check your work?
17. Do you tend to get caught up in details and miss the big picture?

continued on next page

Assessment of Executive Functions

18. Do you anticipate potential problems?

19. Do you have difficulty organizing your thoughts for writing assignments?

20. Do you get stuck when trying to finish work or solve problems?

21. Do you remember what you are supposed to do?

22. Do you get upset easily?

23. Do you have good ideas but have trouble organizing and executing them?

24. Do you know when you need help?

25. Do you ever change topics or strategies in midstream?

26. Do you ever speak impulsively?

▶ **Observation of problem-solving skills**

Conducting an informal observation of a child's ability to solve problems is a rather deliberate process that requires careful planning. Whether you decide to observe the child attempting to solve an unfamiliar/novel task, or whether you determine it is useful to see the child attempt to carry out a functional/life skills task, a few key points need to be considered.

1. For children who have little to no self-awareness, you may need to select a task they claim to be able to execute independently and successfully, rather than one that is completely unfamiliar. If they experience failure, they are likely to rationalize with comments such as, "Well, I couldn't do that anyway" or "I've never done that before, so how do you expect me to know what to do?" It's also important to understand that they probably don't perceive anything wrong with their executive function skills. They will blame the environment, the task, or the examiner when they experience failure instead of the success they so assuredly predicted. For these children, choose a task based on information you have gathered from parents or teachers. You want to be reasonably certain that these children will experience difficulty or require significant help. The point here is to see their efforts in motion and have an opportunity to use the activity to determine the extent of their self-monitoring and evaluation.

Assessment of Executive Functions

2. Conversely, it may be possible to select more novel activities for children who are less prone to argue the definition of "success" with you. These children have poor strategic thinking and demonstrate an inability to plan or sequence steps toward resolution in a situation. They tend to approach novel tasks with a haphazard style that lacks goal-oriented direction. Children with this profile may try the same approach repeatedly, without success or recognition that the strategy isn't working. They may fixate on irrelevant details, overlook critical components and requirements of the task, or become distracted by their own intrinsic interests in the task. As the evaluator, don't intervene; resist the urge to cue or correct. Observe how they approach the task and see how far they are able to go before giving up or requesting help. Even then, you may only want to offer general pieces of advice, such as "Can you think of another way to try it?"

3. An equally important factor to consider is how motivating the task will be to the child. Nothing sabotages assessment faster than a child who finds no inherent value in what you ask her to do. There needs to be some kind of internal motivation for the child to put forth a sincere effort or enough of an external motivation that the child becomes concerned and adopts a sense of responsibility for completing the task. Without a sincere effort, you won't be able to discriminate whether the child has a deficit or a lack of interest, although sometimes severe deficits of initiation are misinterpreted as a lack of interest and effort. Make every attempt to choose activities that match the interests of the child or have some personal relevance to her life.

    In providing external motivation for the task, you might choose to tell the child that "Your friend needs this fixed right away," "The teacher down the hall needs this assembled before her next class," or "Your mom needs these things before dinner tonight." These words of encouragement often hit the right tone with an eager child. Such third-party demands allow you, the examiner, to distance yourself from the task requirements and presumed knowledge of how to complete the task. When expecting your guidance, you can respond with comments such as, "I don't know. It's for Mrs. Miller and I'm not sure how she's done it before. Just try to get it done the best that you can" or "Your mom asked us to get all of these things on her list, but she didn't say where to find them. I hope we can make it there and back with everything." Generic comments like these place the responsibility and motivation for planning, organizing, executing, and adapting on the shoulders of the child.

Assessment of Executive Functions

4. Another aspect to consider when planning functional tasks for life skills is to account for the unpredictability of the real world. As mentioned earlier, therapy rooms are often too sterile and isolated to offer any real sense of the constantly changing environment that we navigate when solving problems, completing assignments, running errands, or managing daily life. Whenever possible, conduct your assessment of functional life skills in the most natural environment possible. Let distractions and interruptions occur naturally. Plan to provide only some of the materials needed to solve novel problems. Impose time constraints similar to what would occur in the child's daily environment. In other words, the only way to observe how well a child adapts, modifies, switches, tunes out distractions, etc. is to incorporate these elements into your evaluation session. The more natural the environment, the less planning you need to do in order to observe how well the child uses executive function skills to flexibly navigate the unpredictability of the real world.

5. Finally, you must be willing to let the child fail. Watching a child try and fail is not an easy thing to do, and it runs contrary to every instinct you have as a parent or professional. It is important not to provide specific cues or answers while the child attempts to work out a plan alone. It is also critical to allow the child's chosen course of action to play out naturally. Your own executive function skills may be screaming at you that the child's strategy will fail, but you must resist the instinctive response to provide assistance that assures success. Making the child aware of potential pitfalls in her plan will eliminate the diagnostic opportunity to observe the presence or absence of self-regulation skills, adaptability, rigidity, perseveration, persistence, etc. Keep in mind that you are watching a process, which is more important than the eventual outcome. You want to know if the child can execute the given task, but more importantly, you want to know whether, and how, the child thinks, plans, strategizes, attends to, and modifies performance along the way. This is the metacognitive blending of language skills with self-regulation to function in the real world.

Examples of functional life-skill tasks and novel problem-solving activities to use in evaluating executive function skills are listed in Tables 4.4 and 4.5 (pages 87-89). Adapt these tasks as necessary to meet the circumstances of your own work environment or the child you are evaluating. You can also modify the difficulty level of the tasks, depending on how subtle the suspected executive function deficits are.

Assessment of Executive Functions

Table 4.4 Sample Functional Tasks for Evaluation of Executive Function Skills

Example Task	Suggested Modifications
Run errands	• Single or multiple errands • With or without time constraints • At actual stores with unpredictable interruptions
Make simple purchases	• For one or multiple items • At one or more places of business • Impose monetary constraints to force anticipation, comparison, etc.
Make deliveries in workplace	• One or multiple items • With or without directions • Require map reading and other navigational skills. • Impose time constraints. • Pre-plan glitches or unexpected additional requests.
Perform simple office tasks	• One simple task or a complex task requiring multiple operations • Give specific or vague directions. • Provide all or some of the materials required to complete the task.
Pack backpack for school or home	• Have the child determine what should go home, as well as organize and pack. • Tell the child what should go home, and let her organize.
Plan class schedule	• For an older child, ask, "What requirements do you have? How many electives can you take? When is lunch/practice?"
Do homework	• Require organization and planning for all homework projects. • Select individual projects and ask the child to execute only that assignment.
Do school project	• Assign the project. • Have the child decide on the project within given parameters. • Provide all, some, or none of the materials required. • Impose time constraints. • Impose distractions and unexpected glitches.

continued on next page

The Source for Development of Executive Functions
Copyright © 2005 LinguiSystems, Inc.

Assessment of Executive Functions

Table 4.4, *continued* **Sample Functional Tasks for Evaluation of Executive Function Skills**

Example Task	Suggested Modifications
Clean room, desk, or locker at school	• Require child to manage laundry, bed, toys, etc. • Have the child manage only one component. • Give specific or vague directions. • Give no directions. • Impose time constraints.
Pack for family outing/trip	• Give the destination and have the child research weather, season, activities, time for travel, etc., and then plan what she will need to take. • Provide the above information for the child, requiring only that she pack items appropriate for the destination. • Use an actual family vacation example, such as an extended trip somewhere, or narrow the focus to a simple day trip to the park.
No-bake cooking projects	• Provide choices for things to make, given a narrow range of food items. • Preselect the item to make. • Give printed or verbal recipes. • Provide all or some of the required ingredients and utensils. • Impose distractions and interruptions.

Assessment of Executive Functions

Table 4.5 Sample Novel Problem-Solving Tasks for Evaluation of Executive Function Skills

Task Category (See *pbskids.org/zoom* for ideas.)	Executive Function Components to Observe (Components of attention, initiation, working memory, and self-monitoring can be viewed in all of these tasks.)
Simple chemistry experiments	• Prediction of outcomes, flexibility, strategic planning, perseveration, impulsivity
Engineering and design projects	• Strategic planning, generating steps and sequences, identifying materials needed, self-monitoring, adaptability
Simple physics, force, and motion projects	• Problem solving when task fails, adaptability, task persistence
Unfamiliar cooking experiences	• Planning steps and sequences, seeking substitute materials as needed
Assembling toys or games	• Impulsivity, pre-planning, attending to and holding in working memory

It would be advantageous to keep a notepad handy to tally the number of opportunities for each executive function skill compared to the number of times the child independently uses that particular skill. This simple chart will allow you to establish a percentage of occurrences for various executive function abilities. The baseline data helps you determine how often an individual uses or misses opportunities to use various executive function skills.

Examples of skills to chart could include the following:

- Establishing goals
- Planning
- Sequencing
- Listing materials needed
- Identifying errors in work
- Correcting errors in work
- Developing alternate strategies
- Using self-talk to modulate work

Assessment of Executive Functions

It's also useful to take note of behavioral characteristics that impede success of a task. Some of those notations could include observation of the following:

- Impulsivity
- Lack of initiation
- Inability to persist with the task
- Inattention
- Perseveration
- Distractibility

Provide additional comments from your informal assessment as to whether the child was eventually able to complete the given task. If so, document if the task was completed independently or with cues, and if it was completed within imposed requirements, such as time limitations. Your baseline data and observations fulfill the assessment goal by providing information on the child's strengths, weaknesses, and strategies that contributed to the ultimate success or failure.

Table 4.6 provides an example of how to break down a problem-solving task into measurable and observable components. It also provides examples of what you might say or do during any given part of the task.

Table 4.6 Informal Assessment of Executive Function Skills—Problem Solving

Component	Example
Establish a required outcome that is relevant to the child's life.	"Today we're going to the convenience store to buy some things. I need two black pens, your mom needs whole wheat bread, and Mrs. Smith wants a local newspaper. Your mom gave us $5 to spend."
Provide time constraints.	"We have half an hour to run this errand. It's 2:00 now, and we have to be back by 2:30."
Deliberately incorporate distracting and unpredictable environments.	Look for nearby places that provide the appropriate environment and that are easily accessible.

continued on next page

Table 4.6, *continued* **Informal Assessment of Executive Function Skills—Problem Solving**

Component	Example
Require multiple accomplishments within the outing.	Have the child find the way out of the building, follow given directions to the destination, manage the money, remember and find required items within the store, monitor time, initiate seeking help when needed, find alternative solutions when necessary, etc.
Ask the child if she needs to plan or prepare.	"Do you need anything before we go?" (something to make a list with, to ask for directions or clarification)
Provide any materials the child may request, but do not offer otherwise.	Paper, pen, maps, etc.
Allow the child to take the lead, directing when and how the task will be initiated.	"I'm ready whenever you are."
Accompany the child during the task as an observer, not as a director.	Plan to take a small notepad and pen, if possible, in order to quickly jot down observations on the number of times the child asks for help, fails to do so when obviously necessary, becomes distracted or off-task, uses unsuccessful strategies, etc.
Avoid offering prompts or pointing out potential problems.	Hold your tongue when you see oncoming problems with task execution. Recognizing and fixing errors is a critical part of the self-regulation process; giving cues prematurely prevents the assessment of this particular executive function skill.
Cue only if and when the child becomes completely unable to continue with the task.	"What should we do now? We need a plan, or we won't be able to get our things and get back in time. Do you need help?"
Allow the child to determine when the task has been completed, even if it is unsuccessful or fails to meet the given requirements.	"Whenever you're done, I'm ready to go."
Evaluate the outcome with the child only after she determines that it is complete.	"How did we do today? Did we get everything on our list? Did we get the right kinds of things on our list? Did you have any trouble? What about your mom's bread—did we buy the bread?"

The Source for Development of Executive Functions
Copyright © 2005 LinguiSystems, Inc.

Assessment of Executive Functions

▶ **Observation of social interaction**

Informal observation of a child's social interaction with peers and adults requires caution on your part as the examiner not to intrude too much into the natural environment. Some children have a tendency to behave somewhat differently when they know that an adult is watching them. Conversely, some children will have little awareness of your presence. Observing the child at school is often the best way to obtain an accurate, well-rounded picture of the child's social, emotional, and behavioral regulation skills. The school environment allows you an opportunity to observe in several environments, both structured and unstructured, such as playground interactions, lunchroom dynamics, and classroom instructional interaction. Generally speaking, deficits in self-regulation fall between two extremes, one of which is the child with little to no impulse control, and the other being the child with little to no initiation or interaction.

> Children described as being behavior problems in school or aggressive in their interactions with others often have poor impulse control.

These children may be driven by intense internal interests that are inflexible to the unpredictability of the world around them. They may have limited recognition of other's facial expression or intonation, limiting their ability to perceive the emotions of others. They often demonstrate a limited range of emotional expression themselves, portraying more black and white ranges of extremes, rather than shades of emotional subtlety.

On the other end of the spectrum are children who rarely initiate social interaction. These children may be viewed as "loners" or socially awkward when compared to their same-age peers. Some children display initiative and efforts to communicate but fail to do so because of impaired social interpretation or inappropriate pragmatic expression. These children may be described as having bizarre interactions, using inappropriate words and intonation to make pragmatic requests. One such child was observed to say "I'm going to cut you to the bone" while apparently attempting to engage another child in joint play on the playground. Not surprisingly, the other child ran away.

The characteristics described relate to the executive function skills regarding regulation of self for socially appropriate behavior. Pragmatic language is much more than the knowledge of linguistic rules to request, deny, convey information,

Assessment of Executive Functions

or converse. The linguistic rule knowledge is fundamental but does not imply the ability to use those rules. Choice and use of verbal information is linked to the perception and use of prosody and facial expression, the nonverbal communication skills that add depth and subtlety to our spoken words.

Interpretation of nonverbal cues must also be learned through experience in social situations. For example, a child learns to interpret that a certain rising intonation connotes questioning, and wide eyes and an open mouth indicate surprise. However, a reliable understanding of these unspoken cues does not equate with an appropriate use of prosody, vocal intensity, or body language. There are also a learned set of behavioral expectations that a child carries with her. Examples include rules for school, home, riding in the car, standing in line, sitting in a movie theater, and so on.

> Learned knowledge of social or pragmatic conventions does not automatically imply consistent or accurate application of these behaviors in functional life situations.

The ability to analyze one's behavior within a social situation, to observe the effects one's voice and mannerisms have on others, to identify when others are hurt or confused by our actions—these are all aspects of self-regulation that require careful attention to subtle cues. But self-awareness is only a part of self-regulation; the rest of the formula requires self-monitoring and self-control or correction. Knowledge becomes the foundation for self-regulation.

Part of your observations need to include commentary on the child's awareness, monitoring, and control with people and the environment. You'll want to evaluate these aspects of self-regulation separately since individual components could be strengths or weaknesses in the child's profile of executive function skills.

Planning a situation to observe social interaction requires consideration of a number of variables. How controlled is the environment? What kinds of interruptions or distractions can be incorporated? Can an element of unpredictability be added to the activity? Will there be other children or adults with whom the child must cooperate? What are the child's interests? Sometimes you might decide to use an activity you know the child is interested in; at other times, you might want to observe how flexible the child can be when faced with topics that are not of interest. As with informal observation of problem-solving tasks, providing some form of internal or external motivation is necessary.

The Source for Development of Executive Functions
Copyright © 2005 LinguiSystems, Inc.

Assessment of Executive Functions

Finally, when planning a social interaction, consider ways to modify the task. Deliberately failing to provide some necessary materials will force cooperation, turn taking, requesting, and impulse control. Imposing time constraints and rules for engagement provide structure similar to real-world tasks and can offer insight into the child's ability to adapt and be flexible.

Table 4.7 presents sample components for informal assessment of social interaction. Modify these examples as needed to fit the profiles of the children you work with.

Table 4.7 Informal Assessment of Executive Function Skills—Social Interaction

Component	Example
Establish a social situation requiring interaction with peers in a flexible, unpredictable situation.	"There's a party for Mr. Walters this afternoon and they forgot the decorations. I wonder what we can make using this box of art supplies?"
Provide task requirements that depend upon teamwork and cooperative interaction to assess sharing and the ability to take the perspective of others.	"If we divide up, we'll get more done. Why don't the three of you take this table, and we'll go to the other one."
Plan to provide slightly fewer materials than children to observe turn taking, inhibition, request making, and impulsive responses.	"We'll have to share because I only have two yellow markers and no green ones. Also, I don't think there are enough glue sticks to go around."
Observe use or absence of social greetings, eye contact, and physical proximity between children.	"Who's at your table, Jeremy?" or "Can I come sit here while I use your paint box?"
Within reason, allow disagreements to occur, and observe if, when, and how the children navigate these conflicts.	"You'll have to work it out between the two of you right now or I'll have to take the art supplies away."
Ask the child how she thinks others feel if and when feelings are hurt.	"I wonder why Ben is crying? Oh, I see. How do you think he feels about that?"

continued on next page

Assessment of Executive Functions

Table 4.7, *continued* **Informal Assessment of Executive Function Skills—Social Interaction**

Component	Example
Impose restrictions to assess adaptability to change.	"The other class needs our beads right now. We'll have to give them the bead box."
Give turns being the leader to observe how children manage having to follow the interests of others.	"I'm sorry, but it's Carson's turn to lead. We must all follow Carson." or "You'll have to leave now. That was your second warning."
Don't allow verbally or physically abusive behavior. Observe how the child reacts; whether the child demonstrates remorse or attempts to rectify the situation.	"Okay, Kate's turn is over. Now it's Mark's turn to tell us his idea." or "No hitting and no yelling in this room. This makes us feel bad and you could hurt someone." or "You are not allowed to grab Margaret's things."
Require inside voices to assess ability to use appropriate intensity. Comment on how a child's prosody sounds to you, observe her reaction, if any, and if she attempts to alter her intonation.	"We have to use our quiet voices inside, especially because we don't want Mr. Walters to know we're making the decorations for his party." or "Jeremy, you sounded angry when you asked for the glitter."
Monitor overall pragmatic use of language rules.	Requests, turns, topic initiation and/or maintenance, denials, comments, interruptions, etc.

▶ **Executive Function Skills Evaluation Worksheet**

An informal outline for evaluating executive function skills is provided on pages 96-99 as an alternative to using a formal assessment instrument. Specific components of executive function skills are delineated, as well as questions to organize your assessment observation. The Yes/No format creates a record of the simple presence or absence of executive function skills, along with an opportunity to comment on the quality of those skills. Use the extra room in the margins to take baseline data for the percentage of occurrence or absence of skills, along with notes characterizing the quality of the child's approach and process. Modify the worksheet as necessary to meet the needs of your particular population.

Observational Worksheet
Informal Assessment of Executive Function Skills

Date _____ Child _____ Age _____

Diagnosis _____
_____

Observational Environment _____
_____

Task Observed _____
_____

▶ **Attention**

1. Can the child focus on the required task? Yes   No

2. Can the child sustain attention to task? Yes   No

   For how long? (record time) _____

3. Can the child selectively attend to relevant stimuli and tune out distractions? Yes   No

4. Is the child able to attend to more than one set of relevant stimuli? Yes   No

5. Can the child shift attention between task components as required? Yes   No

6. Does the child require prompts to pay attention? Yes   No

   How frequently?   Constantly   Periodically   Rarely

▶ **Inhibition**

1. Can the child control impulsive behaviors? Yes   No

2. Does the child require cues to stop talking in order to listen? Yes   No

   How frequently?   Constantly   Periodically   Rarely

Observational Worksheet, continued

3. Does the child stop to evaluate a situation before responding?   Yes   No

4. Does the child plan responses before acting?   Yes   No

5. Can the child delay desirable behaviors until they are required by the task?   Yes   No

6. Can the child inhibit impulsive verbal responses to meet the social criteria of the interaction?   Yes   No

▶ Initiation and Persistence

1. Does the child independently begin tasks or steps to a task?   Yes   No

2. Does the child continue goal-oriented behavior once initiated?   Yes   No

3. Does the child ever become "stuck" mid-task?   Yes   No

4. Does the child require specific verbal prompts to begin or continue efforts? ("Do this, Stand here, Read this" etc.)   Yes   No

5. Does the child require physical prompts to initiate motor activity?   Yes   No

6. Can the child determine whether, and when, his/her task is complete?   Yes   No

▶ Goal Selection

1. Does the child recognize specific directions to execute a task?   Yes   No

2. Does the child identify nonspecific cues from the environment that require action?   Yes   No

3. Can the child select beneficial goals that have outcomes to meet expectations of school, home, or other environments?   Yes   No

The Source for Development of Executive Functions
Copyright © 2005 LinguiSystems, Inc.

Observational Worksheet, continued

4. Does the child select realistic goals that match his/her skill level, time constraints, available materials, and opportunity?   Yes   No

5. Can the child select behaviors that afford long-term rewards, rather than immediate gratification?   Yes   No

▶ Planning and Organization

1. Can the child establish a strategic approach to the problem?   Yes   No

2. Can the child identify materials needed to solve the problem?   Yes   No

3. Can the child identify all the necessary steps required to achieve the desired outcome?   Yes   No

4. Can the child sequence and order the steps he/she has identified?   Yes   No

▶ Flexibility

1. Can the child switch demands for his/her attention from one task to another as appropriate?   Yes   No

2. Can the child adapt a new strategy when previous ones have failed?   Yes   No

3. Can the child adapt a new strategy when faced with a change in the environment or task requirements?   Yes   No

4. Does the child resist prompts to switch his/her approach or to change tasks?   Yes   No

5. Can the child tolerate unexpected intrusions that require a new strategy?   Yes   No

6. If the child can switch focus, is he/she able to return to planning and organizing steps?   Yes   No

Observational Worksheet, *continued*

▶ **Execution and Goal Attainment**

1. Does the child demonstrate deliberate, purposeful effort toward the desired outcome? Yes No

2. Can the child work within time constraints? Yes No

3. Does the child initiate and persist with efforts until a task has been completed? Yes No

4. Does the child persist with ineffective strategies? Yes No

5. Does the child exhibit perseveration? Yes No

▶ **Self-Regulation**

1. Does the child recognize errors in his/her work efforts or social interactions? Yes No

2. Can the child predict outcomes of his/her behaviors, words, or efforts? Yes No

3. Does the child anticipate consequences of ineffective strategies and plans? Yes No

4. Is the child aware of the need for help, cues, guidance, or instruction? Yes No

5. If the child becomes aware of errors, can he/she fix the errors? Yes No

6. Does the child correct errors when given cues? Yes No

   How often are cues required? Constantly Periodically Rarely

7. Can the child recognize errors after the task, given feedback and examples of failed efforts? Yes No

8. If the child can identify ineffective strategies, can he/she stop work to form a new strategy? Yes No

The Source for Development of Executive Functions
Copyright © 2005 LinguiSystems, Inc.

Assessment of Executive Functions

Assessment Case Examples

Problems in the development of executive function skills can occur within a wide variety of disorders. Chapter 3 on co-morbidity includes multiple examples of primary disorder labels that also include deficits in executive function skills as a component of the characteristic profile. In the following section, specific case examples are provided to illustrate the type of assessment data that is typically generated and how it can be used to refine treatment goals. Each case includes background information and data generated from an assessment battery, including both formal and informal evaluation results.

▶ **Child with executive function deficits associated with Williams syndrome** (including ADD/ADHD and cognitive impairment)

Background Information

Matthew was a 15-year-old boy with a moderate language delay and deficits in executive function skills associated with a clinical diagnosis of Williams syndrome. As part of the Williams syndrome profile, Matthew was also diagnosed with attention deficit hyperactivity disorder (ADHD) and mental retardation at a mild-moderate level (educable mental impairment). The hyperactivity and inattention contributed to deficits in communication, behavior, and self-regulation. His rate of speech was quite rapid, and Matthew had difficulty maintaining the topic of conversation.

Matthew's parents noticed delays in his development as early as one year of age. In early years, he demonstrated behavioral aggression, which included head butting, punching and kicking, socially inappropriate physical touching, tantrums, and frequent episodes of crying. Matthew's mother noted concern early on for his impulsivity and seeming disregard for dangerous situations. She also observed a tendency toward affection and cuddling, which at times were excessive in nature.

Matthew's current educational placement was in a cross-categorical classroom, where he had a one-on-one instructional aide. Medications prescribed to address symptoms included 25 mg of Adderall twice daily, 0.2 mg of Clonidine daily, and 25 mg of Impramine daily. Matthew has received speech-language therapy for several years. Previous goals had focused on vocabulary, concepts, language processing, *wh*-questions, sequencing, problem solving, and pragmatic interaction.

Assessment of Executive Functions

In therapy, Matthew was friendly, willing to work hard, and generally talkative. He continued to demonstrate a rapid rate of speech, and inattention and impulsivity in his approach to tasks. As more functional activities were integrated into treatment, Matthew began to demonstrate frequent "shutting down," both physically and verbally. At its worst, Matthew's inability to initiate any motor activity was characterized by the absence of eye contact, tensing of muscles, and silence. Treatment more recently had begun to focus on increasing Matthew's self-awareness, his use of requests for help when needed, his use of self-cued mantras to "stop, think, look at people, talk clearly," and specific work on simple planning and sequencing. In addition, goals addressed speech intelligibility, expressive language skills, and successful task execution, using both communication and executive function skills.

Matthew's parents hoped to help him successfully transition to a high school environment. The school district assured them that Matthew's long-time aide would be retained to follow him to the cross-categorical classroom in the high school. The parents also expressed concern regarding Matthew's ability to reach his functional potential. They wondered how well Matthew would handle daily life skills, safety issues, decision making, self-control, and appropriate social behaviors and communication as he began interacting with typical high-school-aged students. As Matthew gets older and grows bigger, his parents are worried about how to manage his behavior at home. He was still aggressive and impulsive, both verbally and physically, in the home environment. Matthew continued to demonstrate poor judgment and decision making, resulting in the need for a significant amount of external cueing and environmental structure to support his daily life skills, such as getting ready on time, initiating taking a shower or doing homework, and interacting appropriately with family members.

Treatment goals had transitioned to almost exclusively targeting executive function skills. Specific objectives focused on increasing Matthew's self-awareness and self-regulation abilities and improving his functional communication for social, academic, and prevocational skills.

Results of formal and informal testing can be found in Table 4.8 on pages 102-103.

Assessment of Executive Functions

Table 4.8 Matthew's Test Profile

Test	Skills Assessed	Results/Information Acquired
Behavioral Assessment of the Dysexecutive Syndrome in Children (BADS-C)	Executive function components of flexibility, novel problem solving, planning, sequencing, using feedback, following instructions, and presence of perseveration and impulsivity	Scored 3 standard deviations below the mean, with impairments in all aspects of executive function measured by test Observations of performance during subtests included: • Need for maximum verbal cues to initiate action on more difficult tasks • Perseverative efforts on the water test • Inability to independently initiate activity not specifically scripted by test instructions • Unplanned and unsystematic efforts to complete the key search task • Difficulty following directions on all tasks • Lack of planning or concern for rule-breaking during zoo map tasks • Lack of awareness for time constraints on six parts test • Some awareness of mistakes and errors but an inability to self-correct these errors • One spontaneous use of compensatory strategy • Generally well-maintained attention to subtests

continued on next page

Assessment of Executive Functions

Table 4.8, continued Matthew's Test Profile

Test	Skills Assessed	Results/Information Acquired
Dysexecutive Questionnaire (component of the BADS-C)	Identifies four areas of difficulty related to executive function deficits: emotional/personality issues, motivation, behavioral, and cognitive difficulty	Areas of concern noted by Matthew's father included impulsivity, planning problems, euphoria, lack of insight and social awareness, aggression/irritability, restlessness/hyperkinesis, distractibility, and problems with decision-making ability
Informal assessment of executive function skills via functional task planning and execution	Ability to generate a plan and follow steps to purchase school supplies (markers and paper) from a small store	Matthew was unable to independently complete this activity. His plan was erratic and lacked goal-oriented behavior, other than a general idea to walk to the store. He frequently "shut down" (was unable to initiate motor movement or verbal productions) and needed forced-choice options between two simple verb phrases to initiate a next step (e.g., "Take a step" or "Stand here."). Matthew was unable to request help when needed or to execute concrete steps of the task without specific, concrete, verbal direction and physical cueing.
Peabody Picture Vocabulary Test—3rd ed. (PPVT-III), form IIIA	Receptive vocabulary	Received a standard score of 62 and an age equivalency of 7 years, 7 months

Assessment of Executive Functions

▶ **Child with executive function deficits associated with Asperger's syndrome**

Background Information

Ryan was a six-year-old boy diagnosed with autistic spectrum disorder characterized by Asperger's syndrome tendencies with concomitant executive function and pragmatic deficits. Ryan had received speech-language therapy services since the age of two years, when he began to demonstrate a delay in socialization skills and mildly delayed verbal development. At present, receptive and expressive language skills were generally age-appropriate. Articulation skills were mildly delayed, primarily for /l, r, th/, and /l/ blends. In recent years, Ryan's speech therapy goals focused on making appropriate requests, taking turns, sharing, appropriate use of pronouns, conceptual vocabulary, and articulation skills.

Primary executive function deficits were Ryan's inattention to task, poor self-regulation and control of impulsive behaviors, inability to take the perspective of others or to "read" nonverbal communication and emotional expressions, inflexibility and difficulty shifting tasks, inappropriate use and modulation of prosody and vocal intensity, and difficulty regulating impulsive and socially inappropriate behaviors to match his "planned" version of more appropriate behaviors. Ryan takes Straterra to increase his concentration, reduce his activity level, and promote sleep at night.

Ryan's mother expressed concern that her son learn to monitor and control his social interactions with other children at school and home. She was an extremely involved parent, following through with recommendations, therapy techniques, and behavioral shaping. In therapy, Ryan responded well to both positive verbal feedback and to negative consequences for his behaviors, including use of green-yellow-red visual cues to reflect the success or failure of his social interactions and pragmatic communication. Current therapy goals focused on the following:

1. Decreasing the frequency of interruptions
2. Producing a more appropriate voice in both intensity and prosody
3. Taking turns
4. Requesting and sharing
5. Being flexible with other people
6. "Reading" facial expressions and body language
7. Controlling his own emotional expressions

Assessment of Executive Functions

8. Identifying problems
9. Determining a socially sensitive strategy to solving problems
10. Generalizing these skills to tasks that were inherently less interesting to him

Future treatment goals were almost completely devoted to developing executive function skills for Ryan. Objectives included the following:

1. Increasing self-awareness and regulation
2. Controlling impulsivity and interruptions
3. Modifying social behavior to fit changing circumstances
4. Engaging in reciprocal play that is in tune with others' emotions and needs
5. Increasing eye contact
6. Increasing the complexity of problem-solving skills
7. Improving speech intelligibility via articulation and rate production

Results of formal and informal testing are presented in the following table.

Table 4.9 Ryan's Test Profile

Test	Skills Assessed	Results/Information Acquired
Informal observation of social interaction with peers and adults during play-based activities	Frequency, initiation, and appropriateness of requests, greetings, turn taking; controlling interruptions, demonstrating cooperative flexibility, taking perspective of others, modifying communication to fit situation, prosody and intonation, facial expression, comprehension of nonverbal social cues, ability to work and play well with others	Ryan performed best when given structure and opportunities to interact with items of interest to him. He demonstrated inflexibility, outbursts of anger, impulsive and inappropriate verbalizations and vocal intensity when tasks shifted to things he was not interested in. Ryan initially made appropriate requests 60% of the time and took turns 50% of opportunities provided, both given maximal verbal cueing.

continued on next page

Assessment of Executive Functions

Table 4.9, continued Ryan's Test Profile

Test	Skills Assessed	Results/Information Acquired
Informal assessment via problem-solving pictures and situations	Ability to identify other people's emotions and feelings both in situational contexts and based on facial expressions alone	Initial accuracy levels for recognizing emotions from facial expressions was at 67%; ability to identify feelings of others given the context of a situation was 75% accurate. Best responses were for feelings such as "angry" or "happy," while perceptions of more abstract emotions such as "lonely" or "bored" were less accurate.
Test of Problem Solving—Elementary (TOPS)	Ability to use language to think and solve problems	Scored 2 standard deviations below the mean Responses characterized by "I don't know" or silence. Most responses were incomplete or contained irrelevant, vague, and tangential information. Attention and response quality increased when pictures were of interest to Ryan (construction and recycling). Poor outcome prediction and recognition of problems was also observed.
Informal assessment of executive function skills via problem-solving materials and provision of real-life situations	Ability to identify presence of problems and to provide relevant solutions to problems	Able to recognize problems 50% of the time, with better identification if problems were personally relevant or previously experienced Deficits linking others' perspective and feelings as rationale for something being a "problem" Able to generate relevant solutions 67% of the time; errant solutions were characterized as either irrelevant or impulsive and socially unacceptable behavior.

continued on next page

Assessment of Executive Functions

Table 4.9, continued Ryan's Test Profile

Test	Skills Assessed	Results/Information Acquired
Goldman–Fristoe Test of Articulation 2	Articulation during spontaneous and imitative sound productions	Received standard score of 88 (WNL), although response quality diminished when test items no longer included visual stimuli (context-providing pictures)
Comprehensive Assessment of Spoken Language (CASL)—Pragmatic Subtest	Awareness of appropriate language in situational contexts, and the ability to modify this language as necessary	Score also reflected knowledge of pragmatic rules without use of these rules. When not in a formal testing situation, Ryan demonstrated impulsive behaviors and poor self-regulation of emotions and verbalizations, which were inconsistent with his demonstrated knowledge of pragmatic rules of conversation.

▶ **Child with executive function deficits associated with Caffey-Silverman syndrome and ADHD**

Background Information

Alex was an 11-year-old boy who presented with multiple congenital abnormalities secondary to Caffey-Silverman syndrome, which involves thickening of cortical bones and infantile fever and irritability. He demonstrated a moderate receptive/expressive language delay with a severe language processing component and concomitant deficits in executive function skills. Specific deficits observed in the area of executive functions included inattention, impulsivity, distractibility, poor planning and sequencing, impaired problem solving, and poor self-regulation and monitoring. Alex had been receiving speech therapy services since the age of three years, with treatment targeting concepts, language processing, mean length of utterance, articulation, voice, pragmatics, phonemic awareness skills, and vocabulary.

Alex's mother expressed concern regarding her son's inability to learn new information or solve functional life-skills problems. She also expressed concern that Alex was beginning to notice more differences between his thinking and that of other children in his cross-categorical classroom. Her ultimate goals for Alex included the capacity to execute simple, repetitive job skills and self-help tasks in order to maximize his independence in life.

Assessment of Executive Functions

In therapy, Alex demonstrated consistent off-task behavior, inattention to information, reduced working memory, concrete reasoning skills, word-retrieval deficits, and impaired sequencing. He responded well to verbal and gestural cues to stop talking, get ready to listen, repeat information in order to confirm understanding, decide what to do first before acting, persist with thinking and reasoning until a predetermined goal had been reached, and verbal praise for efforts and "good thinking."

Future treatment goals for Alex included the following:

1. Continue work on concrete language processing skills, specifically categorization, organization, word retrieval, and comparison

2. Improve functional expressive communication skills, including simple explanations and descriptions

3. Improve speech intelligibility, using a focus on improved self-awareness and self-monitoring

4. Target specific executive function skills to achieve the following:
   - Increase attention span
   - Decrease impulsive thinking and behavior
   - Increase self-awareness
   - Develop compensatory strategies during functional tasks and social interaction, such as repairing communication breakdowns and requesting more information

Results of formal and informal testing is summarized in Table 4.10 (page 109).

Assessment of Executive Functions

Table 4.10 Alex's Test Profile

Test	Skills Assessed	Results/Information Acquired
Peabody Picture Vocabulary Test-III (PPVT-III)	Receptive vocabulary	Scored 2.5 standard deviations below the mean Alex was observed to occasionally point to a response before the examiner finished stating the target word (impulsivity and poor inhibition).
Expressive One Word Picture Vocabulary Test (EOWPVT)	Expressive vocabulary	Scored 2.5 standard deviations below the mean Alex often used general words in place of specific ("papers" for mail, and "clothes" for luggage).
Behavioral Assessment of Dysexecutive Syndrome in Children (BADS-C)	Executive function components of flexibility, novel problem solving, planning, sequencing, using feedback, following instructions, and presence of perseveration and impulsivity	Scored 3 standard deviations below the mean Alex demonstrated difficulty in all areas of executive functions measured by this test. Performance was worse on tasks requiring more complex rules that also shifted in nature. Inattention, impulsivity, and distractibility compounded these problems. Alex perseverated on the use of ineffective strategies during a problem-solving task even when given cues and hints. His strategy during a search task was unplanned, unsystematic, and random. Rule-breaking and poor attention to time-constraints was observed during other subtests.
Dysexecutive Questionnaire (component of the BADS-C)	Identifies four areas of difficulty related to executive function deficits: • emotional/personality issues • motivation • behavioral • cognitive difficulty	Alex's mother completed the questionnaire, marking areas of concern including distractibility, temper control, and over-excitedness.

The Source for Development of Executive Functions

Assessment of Executive Functions

▶ **Child with executive function deficits associated with a balanced chromosomal translocation, expressive and receptive language delays, and mental retardation**

Background Information

Sarah was a 9-year, 5-month-old girl who had been in speech therapy since the age of 14 months. She was born with a balanced chromosomal translocation that has been associated with developmental delays and mental retardation. She also demonstrated moderate to severe receptive and expressive language delays, as well as deficits in executive function skills.

The diagnostic history on Sarah was fairly extensive over the last several years. Previous speech-language goals focused on the following:

1. Vocabulary
2. Concepts
3. Syntax
4. Language processing
5. Sequencing
6. Describing
7. Following directions
8. Remembering and retelling information
9. Phonologic awareness skills (including sound sequencing, rhyming, sound discrimination in isolation)
10. Syntax development
11. Grammatical understanding

The grocery list of speech-language deficits had never been organized into major segments; everything was being worked on at the same time and with equal emphasis.

In therapy, Sarah was extremely quiet and generally very well behaved. She spoke in a near-whisper, despite frequent cues to "use a louder voice" or "I didn't hear what you said." Receptive language was characterized by the need for frequent repetitions, clarifications, simplifications, and increased response time. Verbal responses were generally one-to-two word utterances, brief phrases, or "I don't know." Closed-ended questions elicited more specific communication interactions than open-ended questions. Visual cues provided a significant benefit, as Sarah

The Source for Development of Executive Functions
Copyright © 2005 LinguiSystems, Inc.

Assessment of Executive Functions

was better able to provide longer sentences and even short descriptions when picture stimuli was presented. In general, Sarah did not initiate conversation; she rarely asked questions and provided only brief responses when specifically asked to do so. When given tasks that she felt were difficult, Sarah tended to shut down, stating "I don't know" or "I can't do that." Significant cueing and encouragement were then necessary to elicit effort toward trying the task. Facial expression was minimal and Sarah's intonation was generally monotone.

Current therapy goals included efforts to improve the following:

1. Expressive communication for simple, short explanations and/or descriptions
2. Auditory attention and verbal memory
3. Language processing and organizational skills
4. Functional communication exchanges
5. Self-awareness and regulation
6. Initiation
7. Simple task completion
8. Use of more appropriate vocal intensity

Sarah's mother expressed her desire for Sarah to eventually be able to try living outside the family home and to develop adequate self-help, communication, and problem-solving skills needed for vocational opportunities. Her parents expressed a desire to help Sarah make the transition from a cross-categorical classroom with first, second, and third graders to one that included fourth, fifth, and sixth grade students. Sarah's mother stated that Sarah often needed help initiating simple tasks, frequently responded with "I don't know," and had difficulty learning information. Her mother also confirmed diagnostic findings of disorganization and poor sequencing, trouble remembering auditory information, and difficulty explaining information and answering questions.

Sarah made marginal progress in recent years with her communication skills. Since Sarah was going to be in the fourth grade next year, a comprehensive assessment of cognitive, communicative, and processing skills was initiated. The tests listed in Table 4.11 on pages 112-114 were administered over the course of an academic year, and were the result of extensive collaboration between speech-language pathology and audiology professionals. These test results were combined with observations of Sarah in therapy and parental report before a summary profile was determined.

Assessment of Executive Functions

Results of formal and informal testing can be found in the following table.

Table 4.11 Sarah's Test Profile (both speech-language and audiology evaluations were completed)

Test	Skills Assessed	Results/Information Acquired
Peabody Picture Vocabulary Test-III (PPVT-III)	Receptive understanding of semantic language	Scored lower than 2 standard deviations below the mean Sarah frequently requires use of examples and more concrete labels to assist her understanding of tasks, questions, and explanations.
Expressive One Word Picture Vocabulary Test (EOWPVT)	Expressive use of semantic language	Scored lower than 2 standard deviations below the mean Sarah's limited expressive vocabulary is felt to be compounded by word retrieval deficits.
Comprehensive Assessment of Spoken Language (CASL)	Comprehension, expression, and retrieval of language in the areas of lexical-semantics, syntax, supralinguistics, and pragmatics	Overall language performance on core and supplementary composites of CASL was within 4 standard deviations below the mean. Significant deficits in the ability to functionally comprehend and use language when communicating with others was indicated, including deficit auditory comprehension, pragmatics, expressive language for both vocabulary and syntax, word knowledge and retrieval, and comprehension of nonliteral information.
Test of Problem Solving—Elementary (TOPS)	Ability to think critically and formulate solutions to problem-solving tasks when supplemented with visual stimuli	Received a standard score below 55 (lower than 3 standard deviations below the mean), indicating deficits in the ability to apply language processing skills to functional problem-solving situations requiring the anticipation of outcomes, organization and provision of solutions, and the identification of relevant information (all components of executive function skills)

continued on next page

Assessment of Executive Functions

Table 4.11, *continued* **Sarah's Test Profile** (both speech-language and audiology evaluations were completed)

Test	Skills Assessed	Results/Information Acquired
Woodcock Johnson–Revised Tests of Cognitive Ability (WJ-R)	Processing speed, visual vs. auditory processing, and fluid reasoning skills	Scored within 4 standard deviations from the mean for Processing Speed cluster Visual Processing cluster score was within 1 standard deviation (SS=91) Auditory Processing subtests scores were greater than 1 standard deviation below the mean (SS=84) Analysis-Synthesis, Concept Formation, and Spatial Relations subtests (requiring fluid reasoning) scores were within 3 standard deviations from the mean A global processing delay in abilities was observed, with relative strengths in pure visual processing.
Behavioral Assessment of Dysexecutive Syndrome in Children (BADS-C)	Executive function components of flexibility, novel problem solving, planning, sequencing, using feedback, following instructions, and presence of perseveration and impulsivity	Scores were below reported norms, with deficits demonstrated in all executive function skills. Of note were Sarah's impulsive responses that lacked preplanning, perseveration on the use of unsuccessful strategies, an inability to use feedback, task impersistence, rule-breaking, and minimal awareness of errors.
Low-Pass Filtered Speech Test	Taxes individual's auditory closure skills (ability to fill in missing components of speech)	Scores were within normal limits for each ear.
Time Compressed Sentence Test	Taxes individual's auditory closure skills and perception of low-redundancy speech	Right ear scores were within normal limits. Left ear scores were slightly below normal limits for Sarah's age.

continued on next page

Assessment of Executive Functions

Table 4.11, *continued* **Sarah's Test Profile** (both speech-language and audiology evaluations were completed)

Test	Skills Assessed	Results/Information Acquired
Dichotic Digits Test	Evaluates binaural integration skills and is less linguistically loaded than other dichotic measures	Scores were below normal limits for age in both ears; a significant discrepancy between right ear (65%) and left ear (30%) was noted.
Competing Sentences Test	Assesses binaural integration, binaural separation, and dichotic listening skills	Sarah could not complete this task using required test procedures. Adjustments to signal-to-noise ratios of competing and target sentences indicated: • Right ear 0% with 10 dB signal-to-noise ratio, 65% with 15 dB signal-to-noise ratio • Left ear 20% with 15 dB signal-to-noise ratio, 25% with 20 dB signal-to-noise ratio, and 80% with 25 dB signal-to-noise ratio
Pitch Pattern Sequence Test	Measures ability to use each ear independently via tones rather than speech, and taxes pitch perception, sequencing, pattern recognition, discrimination, interhemispheric integration, and organizational skills	Sarah could not complete this test, and it was discontinued. She had difficulty with both response types (labeling patterns as low-high-low, high-high-low, low-low-high, etc. and humming the tonal sequence). Visual cues (blocks and hand signals) were not helpful for organizing responses. Deficits were displayed when elements were reduced from three to two.
Duration Pattern Sequence Test	Evaluates temporal patterning using long and short stimuli rather than stimuli that vary in pitch (identical to *Pitch Patterns Sequence Test* except for type of stimuli)	Sarah could not complete the task, and it was discontinued. She could provide responses for two elements but not for the three elements required for test completion.

Assessment of Executive Functions

Sarah's audiological profile revealed a pattern of deficits in sequencing, planning, organizing responses to and acting upon auditory information and instructions. Her performance further deteriorated when speech was presented in noise, and was consistent with associated deficits in word retrieval, organizational skills, motor planning, and difficulty following directions. Sarah's speech-language profile was consistent with moderate-severe delays in receptive and expressive language skills with associated deficits in executive function skills. Sarah's receptive language was characterized by the need for frequent repetitions, clarifications, simplifications, and increased response time. Her expressive communication skills were characterized by simple, concrete, and delayed speech production. Finally, Sarah's executive function skills were characterized by deficits in flexibility, novel problem solving, sequencing, and planning. Work efforts were perseverative in nature, with a lack of strategic planning or goal-establishment. Based on the evaluation results, formal assessment of word retrieval skills was recommended in order to identify the most effective cueing strategies to elicit accurate, efficient responses. Future therapy would focus on the use of communication repair strategies and the use of themes and relevance to link meaning to tasks. Therapy goals for Sarah included the following:

1. Improve verbal organization and working memory
2. Improve attention, processing, and recall of verbal information
3. Increase self-awareness and self-cueing for the following:
   - Using appropriate vocal intensity
   - Asking for help
   - Seeking more information
   - Requesting additional time

A comprehensive list of teaching strategies was also designed for use with Sarah in therapy and in the classroom, which included the use of visual materials, repetition and restating, emphasis of relevant content, and reduction of environmental distraction and background noise to support learning, organization, and output. An FM system was recommended for use in the classroom setting to help Sarah's listening skills in the presence of classroom background noise.

▶ **General Impressions from Assessment Case Studies**

A few common themes run through the case examples provided. Assessment results often produce some discrepancies when executive function deficits are emerging as the primary problem. Some general differences are noted on the next page.

Assessment of Executive Functions

- Contradiction in informal versus formal assessment results
- Contradiction in knowledge versus skills in language assessment
- Contradiction in diagnostic labels

First, formal results are sometimes contradicted by informal impressions. It is not unusual for a child with executive function deficits to know the rule or be able to verbally express an appropriate behavioral response for a social situation, but not be able to actually demonstrate that behavior in real life. Many children with developmental problems in executive function skills have normal intelligence, but need to be told repetitively what they are supposed to do in certain situations. The language knowledge is acquired, but it is not functionally implemented. That is the most important point that becomes apparent in executive function deficits—the difference between knowledge and skills.

The discrepancy between knowledge and skills might be more easily understood in contexts other than executive functions. For example, you could read every book and acquire all the knowledge generated about how to play a musical instrument. But until you apply the knowledge (i.e., demonstrate the actual skill) by producing pleasant sound from the instrument, you are not a competent musician. Competence is based not only in knowledge, but it must be functionally demonstrated in performance of a skill.

Children who fail to develop executive function skills lack the ability to apply knowledge. This information leads to the second impression gained from the assessment case studies. When parents or professionals first noticed developmental problems, it was in the more obvious developmental areas, such as receptive and expressive language or processing. Early intervention goals addressed foundation language skills. As the child grew older, the concrete problems resolved in response to intervention, but the implementation problems remained. Language therapy stopped short of functional carryover, namely executive function skills. Progress was satisfactory in fundamental language objectives, but the residual aspect of executive function skills remained.

Most language problems addressed in therapy will also require some direct treatment on development of executive function skills to generalize and functionally apply the knowledge acquired. In fact, the case studies clearly illustrate how the treatment goals gradually evolved to almost exclusively address development of executive function skills.

Assessment of Executive Functions

Third, almost all of the children summarized in the case studies were initially diagnosed with a more concrete global disorder, such as Ryan with autism characterized by Asperger's syndrome or Alex with ADHD. Executive function deficits commonly occur as a component of other developmental disorders; they are not usually diagnosed as a stand-alone disorder label. That does not mean that executive function skills are not important. They need to be considered and addressed in almost all language-based disorders. Speech-language pathologists conducting assessment need to always evaluate the area of executive function skills and insure that functional application and integration of language knowledge is occurring in the school and home environments.

Summary

The development of executive function skills is critical to effective application of acquired speech-language skills into everyday life. Assessment batteries have tended to focus on isolated communication skills in articulation, hearing, voice, fluency, and language areas (i.e., syntax, pragmatics, morphology, phonology, semantics) without evaluating effective integration of those discrete skills that serve as the foundation for appropriate social interaction and everyday competence. Executive function skills are the gestalt, which becomes more challenging to accurately evaluate and treat. Evaluation instruments to assess areas of executive function were developed first for adults who lost these skills due to brain injury or trauma. As knowledge of developmental disorders increased, professionals began to notice the frequency of poor executive function skills in children. Since that time, standardized assessment instruments have been developed to assist in the evaluation of executive function in children, although most clinicians rely on informal observation and checklists.

Treatment goals should always include generalization into executive function skills. Developing discrete communication skills without integrating them into functional application represents an incomplete intervention plan. This chapter has attempted to delineate specific component areas to evaluate, as well as to provide some guidelines and ideas for incorporating evaluation of executive function skills into an assessment battery. Speech-language pathologists are encouraged to try some of the techniques to add data to the assessment profile reflecting the functional integration of communication skills.

> Conscientious speech-language pathologists have begun to recognize that moving into executive function skills is the final refining step in effective treatment. If executive function skills are not addressed, therapy stops short of a successful conclusion. The challenge becomes how to accurately evaluate the diverse and overlapping aspects of executive function skills.

Chapter 5
Global Treatment Approach

Overview

The development of executive function skills is a critical aspect of effective communication and competence in everyday life. However, executive function abilities require development of very complex and integrated skills. The foundation of discrete skills must be adequately acquired in the many diverse areas of communication, such as articulation/phonology, morphology and syntax, semantics, pragmatics, fluency, processing, etc. Executive functioning involves integration and refinement of those basic communication competencies.

> Deciding how to proceed with intervention for any given deficit will depend upon the nature of the deficit, the degree of functional impairment observed, the immediate needs of the child and his family, or the child's level of linguistic and cognitive ability.

The challenges presented in treatment of executive function deficits are consistent with the complexity of executive function skills. A child with executive function deficits can benefit from a number of different treatment approaches.

The assessment of executive function skills must be thorough and definitive if treatment is going to be effective. It is important to understand the whole picture of executive function skills, both strengths and weaknesses, to appropriately design and conduct treatment. Specific executive function skills might need to be developed, such as self-regulation, but the treatment must integrate those discrete skills into the functional whole. Using the orchestra analogy from pages 8-9, the specific skills for playing an instrument and reading music must be adequately developed. Then the coordination of trained, competent musicians must be refined to create an entire orchestra capable of performing an endless combination of style, rhythm, tone, and harmony.

Treating deficit executive functions requires that the professional look at the overall development of the child. The speech-language pathologist (SLP) must first identify trends in the child's performance across different environments that exemplify executive function deficits identified during assessment procedures. Then the SLP needs to differentiate between impaired primary or secondary processing skills versus impaired metacognitive processing. These variables must be examined so that goals can be established to lay the foundation for long-term internalization and use of well-developed executive function skills.

This chapter will present global treatment approaches for addressing competence in executive functions and to promote the development and use of these highly complex integrative processes. It will also address direct treatment strategies designed to promote the development of specific executive function skills. Usually the treatment for executive

Global Treatment Approach

function deficits will be combined with some form of language therapy, depending upon the nature of underlying linguistic processing disorders.

Treatment for developing executive function skills is multifaceted and not a simple linear plan. The SLP coordinating treatment needs to juggle a number of variables in determining the most effective treatment plan. Some treatment approaches make changes to the external environment, either by providing external cues to elicit behaviors and communication or by altering the nature of the environment to be less taxing on the developing skills. Some intervention approaches strive to alter executive functions themselves, while yet others work to improve the child's ability to cue himself to use newly developed skills or compensatory strategies.

The following diagram illustrates the multiple variables available for consideration in a treatment plan. Each of these variables is discussed in the following pages. Later, the chapter will explain how to blend these options into a viable treatment plan.

Treatment Diagram

Executive Function Skill (e.g., inattention and impulsivity)

- Educating Caregivers and Teachers
- Teaching the Specific Executive Function Skill
- Environmental Modifications
- Lowering/Modifying Expectations
- Increasing Self-Awareness and Self-Regulation
- Compensatory Techniques and Strategies
- Specific Languages/Communication Objectives

The Source for Development of Executive Functions
Copyright © 2005 LinguiSystems, Inc.

Global Treatment Approach

▶ Educating Caregivers and Teachers

One of the most critical aspects of treating deficits in executive function deficits is conveying what the nature of the impairment is to those closest to the child. Parents have often been searching for years for some kind of explanation for the seemingly disparate elements of their child's behavior. The sense of relief and understanding that you, as the SLP, can provide should not be underestimated. The same applies for teachers and other school professionals who work with the child. Just as we would explain the nature of phonological or semantic delays, we must assume responsibility for explaining what deficits or delays in development of executive function skills mean. Parents and other professionals need to understand the impact and ramifications of impairment in this aspect of communication skills.

It is always helpful to rely upon our counseling skills when initially approaching this topic. Many parents have a tremendous amount of emotional investment and years of worrying about how to best help their child become more socially appropriate or behaviorally predictable and reliable. Conversations of this nature can be delicate and demand both professional sensitivity and clarity. Parents and caregivers want answers, but sometimes such complex information can be difficult to internalize. The most effective discussions on this topic link specific examples of the child's behavior to the underlying deficit executive function skill, combined with suggestions for making simple modifications in the environment or using compensatory strategies to offer immediate relief in the home or school.

For example, consider the child who could not sequence to remember the steps involved in taking a shower each day as part of his normal hygiene routine. In addition, he was not able to effectively use language as an internal self-cueing system. The mother of this child expressed fatigue and frustration with the need to tell her son how to complete this process every single night. In discussion, the SLP suggested that the mother make a simple and specific list of the steps she wanted her son to complete for his shower, laminate the sign, and place it on the wall in the bathroom. The child's reading competency was taken into consideration so that an appropriate level of language was used. The child's first experience using the external cueing system was a success, with one exception—the child failed to get a towel out before getting into the shower, and therefore needed help from his mother for that single step. Nonetheless, this was a tremendous improvement over previous nights, and the mother expressed intense relief. A simple revision in the cueing chart added the statement to "get a towel," and from then on, the child executed this life skill accurately and independently.

Global Treatment Approach

The conversation with this mother would have been less useful if the SLP had simply explained the child's deficits, independently developed a strategy, and created the checklist of sequenced steps required for taking a shower. By providing caregiver education and input, the explanation became personalized and resulted in immediate relief in the home through the use of environmental modifications and an external cueing system. The parents also experienced ownership and success in their own personal modifications to address the child's challenges. The development of a more long-term and specific treatment plan to address the child's deficit executive function skills was initiated during speech therapy sessions. In the meantime, the boy's parents experienced firsthand their ability to modify inappropriate behavior to make life less stressful in everyday situations in their home.

It is often helpful to remind caregivers and teachers that while they are working the front line, you will be working with the child to develop the underlying skills and compensatory strategies necessary to promote independence and success. This team approach is certainly the most successful, and it conveys the idea that the teacher or parent is not alone in the process of coping with these functional deficits. Behavioral outbursts, socially-inappropriate comments, or the constant need for instruction and reminders can wear down the most patient people. Acknowledging the efforts of those closest to the child is a critical component of counseling and educating, especially since many children with deficit executive function skills require a tremendous amount of energy, day in and day out, to keep focused and on track with seemingly simple or obvious tasks.

▶ Environmental Modifications

When you observe a child during informal assessment, make careful notes about the surrounding environment. Your written notes might describe the following:

- Amount of background noise that is competing for the child's attention and interfering with processing

- Amount of visually stimulating information present in the environment that might be overwhelming the child

- Presence or absence of physical constraints, such as dividing walls or barriers to offer separate work space

- General number of other children sharing the environment

Global Treatment Approach

- Presence or absence of lists and reminders posted in the child's environmental setting

- Presence or absence of organizational bins or storage units

The structure and organization of the environment will have a large impact on the child's ability to function effectively. If minimal to no structural organization is externally provided, it is completely up to the child to generate his own internal sense of how to organize the world around him. Cluttered environments make the child work much harder to identify priorities, find necessary materials, generate strategic plans, monitor and regulate the quality of work, and maintain focused attention on the task at hand. Disorganized environments also contribute to miscommunication, as distractions tend to disrupt joint interaction and conversation. Children who are predisposed to misreading social and/or nonverbal cues find it even more difficult to make these interpretations when trying to weed out irrelevant and competing stimuli at the same time.

Suggestions for Classroom Environmental Modifications

☐ Provide all the necessary materials for tasks you expect the child to perform independently.

☐ Group similar items together, particularly if they will be used together.

☐ Show the child your organizational system ("All of your blocks are in here, Let's put all of the cars and driving things in this bin," etc.).

☐ Experiment with the amount of art on your walls, particularly in a classroom for children who are easily overstimulated.

☐ Work to balance the amount of white space on the walls of a classroom with the amount of visual stimuli.

☐ Provide labels, lists, and simple signs when appropriate.

☐ Create a flow-plan of how the space is to be used; consider where "quiet" areas will be in relation to "loud" areas.

☐ Make it easy for a child to access what he needs, and limit the amount of distraction that may interfere with success.

Global Treatment Approach

Suggestions for Home Environmental Modifications

- ☐ Eliminate clutter, trash, and unused items.

- ☐ Maintain routine and consistency in the environment; don't let things like clean laundry pile up and interfere with the organizational structure and accessibility of items in a space.

- ☐ Monitor the amount of stimulation on bedroom walls.

- ☐ Provide visual schedules and lists for completing everyday routine chores.

- ☐ Impose external barriers for things the child is not able to internally monitor for himself (e.g., place child-locks on cabinets containing potentially dangerous materials)

If a teacher or parent has provided a maximum amount of visual and physical organization, then the demand on the child is decreased, allowing for more independent success in communicating with peers, learning new tasks, and successfully completing familiar activities.

▶ **Increasing Self-Awareness and Self-Regulation**

The ability to use compensatory strategies to overcome deficit executive function skills, or to consciously apply intact executive function skills to a given situation, requires self-awareness. This does not mean simply paying attention to the task, but rather, implies a metacognitive process of constant self-evaluation and assigning of value judgments to the cognitive and linguistic behaviors being executed. Paying attention to one's performance is only part of self-awareness. Attention to a task without evaluating the quality of work being completed is fairly useless. A child could actually have good attention without being able to recognize the presence of errors or even failure on the task.

Another part of self-regulation is being able to recognize the need to act or behave in a certain manner in the present in order to achieve a desired goal in the future. Self-regulation is dependent upon the ability to be aware of one's actions and to apply some value judgment on the quality of work or communication put forth.

Global Treatment Approach

Regulating behaviors is a separate skill designed to meet a long-term desired outcome and requires inhibition or initiation in order to alter words and actions accordingly. A child could demonstrate impaired self-regulation at a number of different levels.

During assessment, you may observe that the child lacks awareness of his efforts, even when others perceive obvious disorganization, impending failure, or offensive social interaction. Or perhaps the child can reflect on his performance but does not have the capacity to evaluate the implications of his efforts, either for achieving an eventual outcome or to prevent disruptive interaction. Finally, you may observe that a child is able to reflect on performance and behaviors, assign correct value judgments to these efforts, and is aware of the need to alter plans, but is unable to modify his performance or communication to fit the desired change. This may be due to an inability to stop failed efforts (perseveration), difficulty generating alternative strategies, or an inability to initiate new efforts.

> The capacity of a child to be aware of and to regulate behaviors is fundamental to the generalization of other skills targeted in therapy, whether it is a specific language goal or an executive function behavior.

In fact, the generalization of any skill is dependent upon self-regulation. One cannot learn a skill and then determine when and how to use the skill without self-awareness and self-regulation. Any good treatment plan needs to take into account how to promote generalization, even in children who have no executive function deficits and who self-regulate quite easily. Learning any aspect of effective communication requires the eventual use of these skills in the child's daily environment. As SLPs, we are already in the business of teaching transition and generalization. In the case of children who present with deficit executive functions, the internalization of skills and responsibility for appropriate use of metacognitive skills is likely to be even more difficult. As such, it must become a direct component of the treatment plan.

Many adults with an acquired injury to the prefrontal cortex are unable to identify errors in their performance, despite what others would consider obvious failures and gross inaccuracies in their efforts. Many of these individuals will seem to be in a state of denial about their deficits. They may attempt to argue or persuade family members and therapists that there is nothing wrong with them or that they do not require assistance and supervision.

Global Treatment Approach

In traumatic brain injury literature, the redevelopment of self-awareness following an injury to the frontal lobe of the brain is broken down into three phases (Barco et al. 1991):

1. **Intellectual awareness** refers to being able to acknowledge that perhaps "something" is wrong with one's ability to perform tasks that were executed independently pre-injury. Often, it takes a tremendous amount of demonstration and presentation of convincing evidence for an individual to begin to recognize his deficits. It is often helpful, and even necessary, to set up a "planned failure" task in which you provide the individual with a task he claims he can do successfully and independently. You should be fairly certain that the individual will actually fail in his efforts. Videotaping the process may be very useful as well to provide the individual with hard-core evidence of his impairments. Providing what is often painful information in such a direct manner is necessary given that many of these patients cannot process subtle or indirect information. Re-establishing self-regulation cannot proceed without the individual's intellectual acknowledgment that there are general deficits to work on.

2. **Emergent awareness** describes the condition of being more directly aware of specific deficits, whether they are in memory, language, reasoning, planning, etc. It is common practice in treating individuals with acquired brain injuries to repeatedly list what therapy they are in, what they are working on, and why. You must be clear, consistent, and able to communicate potentially devastating information in a sensitive, yet firm, manner. Individuals with an emergent awareness of their inability to perform daily life skills, such as dressing, walking, driving, reading, or remembering, are likely to express a wide range of emotions as they begin to internalize this knowledge.

   Yet the increased awareness is vital if the individuals are to regain the ability to apply compensatory strategies, use environmental cues, relearn specific skills, or begin to internally cue themselves for improved performance. It is often said that a person can't sincerely address a problem until he is willing and able to acknowledge that there is a problem that needs to be addressed.

Global Treatment Approach

3. **Anticipatory awareness** reflects a level of awareness that promotes the anticipation of difficulty in applying a relearned skill or compensatory strategy or using an external cueing system to overcome the deficit. Without the ability to anticipate some type of difficulty, there is no generalization. Skills learned in a controlled environment are only as good as how they are applied in a non-controlled environment. The unpredictability of real life demands constant self-appraisal and application of any number of skills and strategies to communicate effectively or perform life tasks. Independence, safety, social interactions, and vocational and academic success all rely on the capacity of an individual to appraise his behavior, identify the need to adapt, and then initiate doing so.

The importance of self-awareness cannot be stressed enough. Self-regulation is dependent upon a child's ability to form accurate impressions of his actions and words. An even worse scenario is the complete lack of self-appraisal. Any treatment plan for executive functions must take into account these skills. The ultimate outcome of a child's goals will only be as effective as their application, based on the internal direction the individual is able to provide.

Ask the children on your caseload why they are in speech therapy. No matter what the goal, each child should be able to answer this question with at least some fundamental, basic understanding of the purpose of treatment. In order for any treatment to be successful, a child needs to understand both the skill and strategy he is working to develop, as well as the implications it will have on his communication or behavioral interactions. Listen to the quality of responses your children provide. Can they tell you one goal they have? Two goals? No goals? If you point out their deficit problem-solving strategies or inaccurate social perceptions, can they acknowledge this, or do they argue the point with you? These are some of the considerations we need to make as professionals if we expect our clients to truly make functional, real-world improvements.

> Do not underestimate the capacity of even very young children to understand what you are teaching them.

▶ Compensatory Techniques and Strategies

Their understanding of the deficits can become the underlying, internal motivation for many children—the knowledge that they are working on something, they come to speech for a reason, and they have the capacity to affect some kind of change in their own lives.

Global Treatment Approach

Once a child can state the basic reasons for attending speech therapy, he is ready to learn how to accomplish his goals.

The use of compensatory strategies may be an endpoint for therapy, or it may be a temporary stop-gap measure to be used while the child works on developing better skills. Unless your data indicates that a child can accomplish a given task independently, that is, without cues or prompts of any kind, then the child is still relying on externally driven help or supervision to elicit an internally generated process. One way to bridge the gap between these two extremes is to give the child a way to compensate and to teach him how to self-cue the strategy.

Most of us probably talk to ourselves at least once during the course of a day, whether silently or out loud, to help prompt memory, organization, sequencing, and to double-check the quality of our thinking. In fact, this is probably the most common example of how people normally use compensatory self-talk to organize, shape, and modify higher-order processes such as problem solving, learning new information, or managing multiple demands within a day.

Strategies improve the quality or efficiency of executive functions by cueing behaviors, halting action until appropriate, sequencing steps, talking through the quality of efforts, keeping a focus on our efforts, etc. Language is the abstraction by which we express our thoughts. Language is the tool we use to qualify our efforts and to represent ourselves to others in a socially recognized manner. We combine language with executive functions to achieve the most independent and successful outcome possible.

> In general, compensatory strategies for executive functions are language-mediated and language-activated.

The specific executive function skill that limits a child's success must be identified before an effective compensatory strategy can be determined. A good evaluation should result in isolating these skills. For example, a child who cannot execute simple homework tasks may not be able to do so because he has poor planning in the steps and sequences to approach the task. When working on teaching the specific skill of identifying what to do first, second, last, and so on, the child may benefit from the immediate use of organizational structures to make him more independent. Developing a checklist, for example, might facilitate organization so the student can complete a worksheet with less help.

Global Treatment Approach

A list including the steps to the right could be generated.

For a child who cannot initiate a plan, teaching a simple cue might help prompt the execution of preplanned steps, such as "Now, start my work." Perhaps the child who cannot initiate a task needs a physical cue to prompt motor actions to execute what has already been independently planned.

> **Sample Checklist**
> ☑ Write my name at the top.
> ☑ Read the directions.
> ☑ Identify the task.
> ☑ How many blanks are there to fill in?
> ☑ Where do I get the answers?
> ☑ Start with number one, then number two, etc.
> ☑ Work until all the blanks are filled.
> ☑ Double check my work.

Although it is externally given, a physical cue is sometimes much easier to give if it helps the child work independently. For example, lead the child to the task and put the pencil in his hand.

Compensatory strategies can be used either short or long term. They may be a temporary means to an end, used only while the child is learning to self-regulate by mastering a developmentally appropriate executive function skill. If a child has reached his potential for a given executive function skill, the use of a compensatory strategy might be a long-term need.

For example, teaching a child with a moderate-to-severe expressive language organization impairment to use a statement such as "I need more time, I need help," or "I need a word" will communicate that the child is trying. Teachers and parents respond much better to this behavior than silence, a shoulder shrug, or "I don't know." Every effort should be made to internalize the strategy so the child achieves a sense of independence with the behavior or communicative interaction.

▶ Specific Language/Communication Objectives

It is typical for children with delays in the development of executive function skills to also present with specific deficits in core speech and language skills. A student with difficulty processing/attaching meaning to auditory information is also likely to have executive function deficits. A student with significant problems in verbal discourse may also experience problems in executive functions.

Global Treatment Approach

While it is important to assess developmental executive function skills, you must also evaluate developmental speech and language skills. If significant processing deficits are part of a child's profile, then you must address those language skills before expecting to realize any significant improvement in executive functions. For example, if a child has deficits in problem-solving skills, such as identifying the problem, generating solutions, choosing the best alternative, etc., he must understand those basic language concepts before he can demonstrate functional problem solving in everyday life. Acquisition of specific speech and language skills are prerequisite to the ability to integrate them into a functional whole.

Why are those foundation skills prerequisite? Neurology provides the clearest answer. Sensory stimulation is channeled to the appropriate lobe of the brain to process—auditory input to the temporal lobe, visual input to the occipital lobe, and tactile information to the parietal lobe. The sensory input is then processed. Once the input is meaningful information, it is integrated with stimulation from the other lobes (visual with auditory) and sent to the frontal lobe and motor strip to formulate a response. The neurological flow of sensory input moves from the sensory lobes into the frontal lobe for more complex processing, planning, and organization of a behavioral response—gestural, motoric, or verbal.

> If inaccurate or incomplete information is sent to the frontal lobe, it is a foregone conclusion that the executive function response will be faulty.

The orchestra analogy on pages 8-9 highlights this idea. A child cannot adequately contribute to an orchestra if he doesn't yet have the skills to play a musical instrument. The foundation communication abilities must be addressed to some degree before an integration of those skills can be expected in executive functions. However, this shouldn't necessarily preclude working on the development of executive function skills at the same time as specific speech-language skills. Sometimes the specific communication skills will develop simultaneously with executive function skills. The purpose for developing the speech-language skill is to insure functional success with that skill through executive functions.

Specific speech-language objectives can, and should, be part of a treatment plan for a child with delays in development of executive function skills. The critical aspect is to weigh and balance treatment expectations. Goals in the area of phonology may have minimal impact on executive function goals, while language processing goals could have a dramatic impact. Coordination of specific communication area goals should be considered when addressing deficits in executive function.

Global Treatment Approach

▶ **Lowering/Modifying Expectations**

The development of executive function skills is an ongoing process that is constantly being updated and modified as new opportunities, expectations, and responsibilities enter a child's life. Parents and teachers don't expect a three-year-old to have the impulse control and patience to sit quietly and listen to someone talk for over an hour. Yet when a child enters elementary school, that expectation is there. The organization strategies required to independently complete a book report are not expected in kindergarten, but they are by third grade. Parents don't trust a child to ride a bicycle in the street at age four, but they do by age seven.

The process of developing the critical thinking, reasoning, and focus to accomplish more functional independence evolves over time. The development of these executive function skills is also dependent on a number of other prerequisite skills. As much as a parent or teacher might desire a specific behavioral response from a child, you must determine if the child is capable of that response at any given point in time. An example to illustrate this idea might help.

If a parent wants her child to be a professional basketball player, she might lecture him over and over on good ball-handling skills, tell him repeatedly of the mechanics involved in a certain type of shot, and have him watch hours and hours of professional basketball on television. But if the child doesn't have some basic fundamental skills, those efforts are premature and not a good use of time. In fact, the child and the parent will quickly become frustrated because their investment of time and effort will not be successful without some prerequisite skills. The child needs to learn to dribble the ball, stand and shoot the ball, and then run and shoot the ball. He needs certain innate skills of motor coordination, physical height, and muscle strength. He needs to make a commitment to motorically practice these skills over and over until the basics become automatic; then finesse and strategy can be added.

A child who is five feet, three inches tall is not a good prospect for professional basketball. A child who has mild cerebral palsy with muscular coordination and strength issues is not a good prospect for professional basketball. A child who is mentally impaired and cannot understand the rules and strategies of the game is not a good prospect for professional basketball. Parents need to be realistic and understand what the capabilities and future prospects for success might be for their child. In the cases cited, the expectations need to be modified.

Global Treatment Approach

Different career choices, such as in a neighborhood or school basketball league or as a team statistician or manager rather than a player, become viable options for the child who does not possess the basic prerequisite skills to become a professional basketball player. While there will be some disappointment, the end result will be more fulfilling for everyone involved.

You might need to assist a teacher or parent in understanding what the current realistic expectations should be for a child in regard to his executive function skills. There might be a behavior that parents or teachers want the child to be able to do responsibly and independently, but the child is not ready to accomplish that task; there are others that must be successfully attained before that skill will be acquired. Using the assessment hierarchy can help you explain this information to parents and teachers, and sometimes the child, so that unrealistic expectations aren't unfairly imposed.

As the professional involved in addressing development of executive function skills, realistically evaluate the child and determine the level of current functioning, as well as a projected future level of functioning. It is important to work in a progression, rather than jumping all over and training specific desired skills in no apparent order. A compromise can usually be generated that meets the desire of the parents or teacher while not imposing unfair or unrealistic expectations on a child with deficits in executive function skills.

Some general strategies to follow when determining if expectations need to be modified or lowered are listed below.

- Carefully evaluate the task that the child is not achieving successfully. A task analysis helps everyone understand the complex variables involved in any perceived "simple" task.

- Determine steps that are being completed successfully and steps that are being missed or executed poorly.

- Modify the expectation on steps being missed. This could entail adding a cue or prompt that is visual, physical, or verbal. Externally reinforce at the point where the child starts to fail.

Global Treatment Approach

- If the task sequence is too complex, break it into smaller tasks that are shorter duration and more likely to be accomplished.

- Gradually fade external cues or prompts to determine if the skill has been internalized. If the child fails, then maintain external assistance and lower expectations.

Two examples of how to modify expectations follow:

1. Parents want their child to independently get ready for bed in the evening. This task includes taking a shower, brushing teeth, and putting on pajamas. The parents might be frustrated that the dirty clothes are always left on the floor rather than put in the hamper. Modifications could include a sign or reminder in the bedroom where the child takes off his clothes or above the pajama drawer to make sure dirty clothes are in the hamper. Another modification would be to break down the whole process of getting ready for bed into three tasks: taking a shower, brushing teeth, and changing clothes. Each task could have a separate external cue sheet so the total isn't so overwhelming.

2. A teacher might want a child to independently get ready to go home in the afternoon. This task involves writing down assignments, taking home the necessary books and materials, and packing his backpack. Again, the multiple sequenced process might need to be broken down into three separate tasks: writing down the assignments, finding the necessary materials, and then preparing the backpack. Modifications within those tasks could include a checklist with all subjects listed. The child simply needs to circle the subjects that have homework and then write in that assignment in the designated space rather than starting from scratch.

The typical process usually starts with modification to accomplish the task. If modifications are not effective, then it might be necessary to lower the expectations as to how much you expect the child to complete independently. The ultimate goal is for the child to experience success while reducing frustration on everyone's part.

Global Treatment Approach

▶ **Teaching the Specific Executive Function Skill**

Treat the source of the problem, not just the symptoms. While this may seem an obvious statement to make, it is critical nonetheless. You must be able to identify which executive function skills are deficit in the child, as well as which skills appear to be relatively intact. You must also decide on what kind of hierarchy for treatment goals makes the most sense for this child.

These questions can be answered after completing a good inventory of executive function skills during the assessment process. "Are the foundation skills of attention and working memory impaired? Do higher order self-regulation skills of monitoring and correcting efforts need to be addressed? What kind of organizational skills does the child have intact?" The table of executive function components, page 15, attempts to separate these aspects into "discreet" skills, while also placing them in a relative hierarchical list. We use the word *relative* here, since the process of applying knowledge to a given situation is fluid with various executive functions overlapping and interacting with one another.

Often the most useful way to answer the questions of which executive function skills are deficit is to ask yourself *why* the diagnostic task or interaction is failing. "Is it because the child is easily distracted and impulsive? Did the child fail to understand the purpose of the conversation or assignment in the first place?" If so, efforts beyond that point are bound to fail. Or maybe the child has excellent attention and can inhibit impulsive responses but is unable to determine where to start, how to sequence ideas, and cannot break the task down into manageable steps for execution.

Some children can do all of the discrete components well but are unable to initiate the effort or verbal interaction to reflect their internal organization and intent. Other students may demonstrate deficits that are apparent only when faced with unexpected changes or expectations but do well when allowed to function within their own regimented routine. In the latter case, the child's inflexibility is likely to reveal perseverative behaviors that lead to failure because he is unable to shift his attention or efforts accordingly.

Global Treatment Approach

Some children do quite well using their executive function skills for thinking and problem solving but demonstrate poor self-regulation for emotional interactions and cannot process social information. Their behavior with others may reflect inappropriate communication and lead to confusion or alienation.

> You need to identify the weak skill and then establish a treatment plan to work on that specific component.

In order to do this well, however, the child needs to understand what he is working on and why, which ties into elements of teaching self-awareness and regulation. Plan to provide the child with specific opportunities to work only on one or two executive function skills within a chosen activity. For example, a child may be able to attend to a task and initiate efforts but does so without first forming a strategic plan, does not sequence or identify relevant steps to take, and impulsively talks about off-topic information during the task. Focus treatment efforts on teaching the child to inhibit efforts until he is able to state a plan, to identify and sequence the steps to take, and to redirect his language toward the plan he has devised.

You would not, in this case, ask the child to work on increasing his attention or working memory. Nor would you focus efforts on the skill of identifying errors. This child's therapy plan would stick to inhibition, sequencing, and task-relevant conversation skills. Goals may include teaching the child to use self-talk to hold off working on a task until he has been able to write down and sequence his plan. "Stop, think, plan, do" may be a useful way to approach inhibition. Before the child is able to internally cue himself, however, you will likely be the one imposing restraint, either by withholding materials needed to initiate the task or by using verbal and physical cues to delay efforts until a strategy can be verbalized.

Efforts to teach specific executive function skills may require a lengthy treatment period, and they certainly require some degree of patience from all involved. As a child begins to demonstrate improved quality of executive functioning, fade external supervision and cueing. Place more responsibility for the skill with the child until the skill has been internalized for a given set of circumstances. At that point, focus therapy on generalizing the executive function skill to a variety of environments and activities, which may mean a temporary return to external cues.

The Source for Development of Executive Functions
Copyright © 2005 LinguiSystems, Inc.

Global Treatment Approach

There is one final consideration for designing therapy to address specific executive function skills. It is difficult to say whether the repetitive practice of any particular skill, such as working on inhibiting impulsivity, actually improves the skill or whether increased awareness and deliberate use of compensatory strategies becomes internalized, thus resulting in a better functional outcome. Additional ideas for developing some of the specific executive function skills will be provided in the next chapter. We will also revisit the case studies presented in Chapter 4: Assessment, adding the treatment plans for each individual case.

▶ Blending the Treatment Options into a Cohesive Plan

Creating a treatment plan to address deficits in executive function skills requires an integrated approach that blends many, if not all, of the processes delineated in the diagram on page 119. The development of executive functions is a process that culminates in independent living, vocational success, and social integration with a community. Therapy goals need to encompass both immediate and long-term needs, with the ultimate goal being that the child is able to manage the most complex level of functional skills possible with the most independence possible.

> Recall the parents of Sarah, who hoped that someday Sarah would be able to live outside the family home. This is a goal whose roots lie in small steps taken in early years. The developing language skills must be blended with developing frontal lobe skills to create a functional person who can evolve into an independent member of society. How well we teach someone like Sarah to use a simple request for more time or more information, or to learn and retain a set of steps required to solve a simple problem, may mean the difference between self-sufficiency and dependence upon her family for the rest of her life.

Generally, the objectives of a treatment plan are formed during the evaluation phase, similar to the assessments we complete for vocabulary, phonology, or syntax. The more skilled we become at the evaluation of deficit executive functions, the easier it is to identify the specific skills we need to address. Careful delineation of executive function skills leads to well developed treatment plans for therapy. Just as the assessment must go beyond delineation of specific skills into functional evaluation of integrated communication abilities, the treatment plan must address both specific skills and their integration into functional life settings.

The Source for Development of Executive Functions
Copyright © 2005 LinguiSystems, Inc.

Chapter 6
Functional Strategies and Goals

Overview

Based on clinical experience, deficits in executive functions respond to different combinations of treatment approaches. Some areas respond well to increasing self-awareness and providing compensatory strategies that the child can use to overcome inefficient means of responding. Other areas respond well to changes in the way information is provided, combined with modifications within the environment. Teaching and repetitive drill of specific skill sets are the best way to address some aspects of executive functions, so the child learns how to respond or think in functional situations.

The approach to developing treatment is dependent on our understanding of **what is wrong** and **why**. This reinforces the necessity of careful assessment to delineate which areas of communication skills (primary, secondary, or tertiary processing) require intervention. As speech-language pathologists (SLPs), we are ideally positioned to combine our knowledge of the child's language skills with executive function abilities to help the child achieve her potential. But we cannot successfully accomplish this without first considering **what** we are working on, **why**, and **how**.

- **What?**

  The **what** should delineate the specific executive and/or communicative skills and abilities that are lacking or have not developed adequately in the child. This is where a thorough evaluation and keen observational skills come into play. Our understanding of **what is wrong**, based on our observations and evaluations of the child, can help to explain **why** the child is experiencing daily failures.

- **Why?**

  The **why** should reflect the child's functional failures in global environments, such as social breakdowns at school or home, inability to develop independent self-care skills, and ineffective thinking and learning skills for academic or prevocational success. The **why** of treatment often becomes apparent from conversations with parents or teachers who experience a child's poorly developed skills firsthand.

- **How?**

  The **how** of a treatment plan must reflect a consideration for the child's primary disorder—the diagnosis that accounts for the presence of the developmental executive function deficits. The chapter on co-morbidity includes examples of several disorders whose characteristic profiles include deficits in executive functions. The treatment approach we design must be consistent with the techniques that are successful within the child's primary disorder.

Functional Strategies and Goals

These treatment variables—**what**, **why**, and **how**—need to converge in well-written goals. Writing goals in a measurable, accountable style is a learned skill; practice and opportunity foster growth and improvement. Goal writing should not become a stagnant part of our work. It should expand with our clinical skills and knowledge, particularly as we employ new understanding and techniques within our practice. Goals that reflect only the **what** of treatment, without consideration for the underlying **why** and **how**, will ultimately fail. Just as we need to understand the features of a class of sounds for designing a valid cycle approach to address phonological deficits, we must also understand the features of executive function deficits in order to write goals and treatment plans that will successfully overcome current deficits, promote continued development, and maximize a child's future potential for independence in life.

Goals can be written to include a focus on the underlying deficit. This is useful since it emphasizes the **reason** a child is unable to carry out a particular activity. Language development might be adequate, but a child may still be unable to successfully follow classroom directions due to impairments in attention and working memory. This child's goals may need to reflect a combination of variables, including use of focused/directed listening, dependence on external cues to focus attention, monitoring length and complexity of information to process, graduated degrees of accuracy, and gradual increases in length of time that the child is expected to maintain attention to task. In addition, the manner in which information is presented might need to be adapted to foster better comprehension and memory.

This chapter provides specific examples of goals that have been used for specific clients with actual deficits in language and executive functions. For goals to be effective, they should blend easily measurable, functional outcomes with the underlying cognitive or linguistic process upon which the desired behavior is dependent. Goals should also include the type and amount of external cueing required for desired outcome in a specified environment. Environmental variables to consider and manipulate include structured/unstructured and distracting/nondistracting.

Consider the following goal:

> *"The child will demonstrate attentive listening in structured environments by demonstrating adequate processing and comprehension of simple directions needed to complete academic tasks, given moderate amounts of physical and verbal cues, with 80% accuracy."*

Functional Strategies and Goals

Whew! Sounds like everything is covered, right? Well, let's analyze the goal a little further. What is attentive listening? Define what is meant by a structured environment. What kinds of verbal cues and prompts? The specific aspects of the child, her disorder, and treatment strategies have to be incorporated into the goal if implementation is going to be successful. In this case, the child presents with ADHD, impulsive responses and actions, and poor attention to auditory information, concomitant with language processing deficits. **Cues** for this child include the specific, direct verbal prompt to "get ready to listen." Gestural cues are useful as well to nonverbally remind the child to hold responses until the desired moment, while encouraging processing time before initiating an activity. **Attentive listening** can be as simple and obvious as priming the child's attentional system to receive information, such as "Be quiet and get ready to listen. I'm going to tell you something important; here are the directions." A **structured environment** for this child is one in which the amount and type of distractions are controlled and predictable. These are the necessary foundations upon which language processing can take place. Writing a goal without these considerations assumes the child can internally mediate attention, working memory, and impulse control. The **goal** may be to facilitate language processing so that the child's comprehension of a message is accurate, but it will certainly fail if we do not lay the foundations of attention, self-regulation, and planning (executive functions) for the desired response.

Global treatment strategies were introduced in Chapter 5. Those over-arching concepts need to be incorporated with the information presented in this chapter, which addresses the development of specific executive function skills.

The goals listed in each of the following sections are appropriate as a starting point for developing specific executive function skills. They are provided as examples of goals we have used with various students over the years. Sometimes the goals include wording to cue a decrease in the rate at which you present information, vary intonation, or emphasize nonverbal communication cues. The goals are not in a hierarchy; they are simply a starting point to assist in constructing goals and designing treatment plans to address specific executive function skills. Sections covered are listed to the right.

Sections Covered
▶ Attention deficits
▶ Impulsivity/poor inhibition
▶ Self-awareness and self-monitoring
▶ Flexibility
▶ Goal selection
▶ Initiation
▶ Perception and expression of social and environmental cues

Functional Strategies and Goals

Attention Deficits

Deficits in attention can impact the effectiveness of social interaction, problem solving, retention of new information in short- and long-term memory, and general learning. Effective attention has broad implications for overall academic and vocational success. Children who present with limited attention spans often require extensive amounts of external cueing in preparation to listen, work, and think. Their ability to internally direct attention is often erratic at best. When combined with hyperactivity and impulsivity, the end result significantly limits the quality of linguistic or cognitive processing.

It takes a considerable amount of self-regulation to focus one's attention. Circumstances in the real world require that a child alternate between competing interests or divide attention among simultaneous tasks. A child must be able to direct sufficient attention to relevant information or effort, while maintaining vigilance to uphold the quality of effort long enough to complete the task. This skill can be particularly important for time-sensitive activities or tasks where the requirements change unexpectedly.

The ability to carry out instructions or retain information accurately is also based in attention skills. Memory for information is partially dependent upon the ability to selectively attend to relevant stimuli long enough to allow for the processing of information. Further attention must be given to the processed information so it can be held in working memory (i.e., immediate store of information from which we make mental manipulations) for immediate manipulation or stored for later retrieval. The quality of attention to information presented has a significant impact on the accuracy of what is stored in memory for later use.

> The main point of therapy is to establish a reliable base of attention first, before providing input to process or act upon. Initially, this may mean imposing some form of external structure for the child, such as positioning her and giving her physical cues to listen. It also may mean altering the environment to be less distracting.

Once a child can attend long enough to receive incoming information, whether visual or auditory, the capacity to retain this information in her mental "space" must be sufficient so that she can make comparisons, conclusions, or decisions. Inattention ultimately interferes with tasks such as conversation, following instructions, learning new information, and heeding warnings or rules; all of which are critical to self-sufficiency.

The Source for Development of Executive Functions
Copyright © 2005 LinguiSystems, Inc.

Functional Strategies and Goals

▶ Environmental Modifications for Attention Deficits

For children who demonstrate both visual and auditory inattention, consider the "loudness factor" in the child's room, classroom, or homework space. Classrooms are often intentionally designed to stimulate imagination and promote thought and learning. However, for a child who is easily distracted or who has a very short attention span, these classroom enhancements can make it impossible to concentrate for very long. Children with messy rooms, desks, and backpacks have that much more to sort through before finding what they need. Lack of organization unnecessarily taxes both attention and patience. The child cannot find what she needs, cannot focus long enough to devise a plan to look systematically for the item, or is distracted by unrelated items in the space. As a result, the child will automatically lose whatever attentional focus she may have had to begin with.

> Simply clearing an environment of unnecessary clutter and placing things in an orderly and visually structured manner can be helpful.

Children who are disorganized and have to consciously focus their own internal thoughts need to be able to access information from their external environment as easily as possible. Montessori classrooms are an excellent example of this principle. Work surfaces are generally free of clutter. Storage shelves contain neatly placed baskets and other containers that hold items of similar size, placed in proximity to items of related use. Principles of order extend into expectations of children in that environment. Students are taught to put their work back into its proper place as part of the learning exercise itself. This reliable sense of organization helps promote clear thinking and exploration of the learning concepts introduced without having to "work" to access materials.

The same principle applies to a child's home environment. Keeping a room free of distracting clutter is much easier when storage solutions and space are readily available. Asking a child to clean up her room becomes an easier task when things have a place. "Everything in its place and a place for every thing" may be something you've heard, and its wisdom holds true. Advising a parent to provide storage containers for things like pencils, rulers, scissors, calculators, disks, or computer-related equipment can be a very simple but effective way to eliminate distractions.

Functional Strategies and Goals

☑ **Quick list of environmental organization to promote attention:**
- ☐ Insert organizational storage space.
- ☐ Sort like items into same spaces.
- ☐ Sort by function, need, frequency of use, etc.
- ☐ Post visual cues (signs, lists).
- ☐ Eliminate visually distracting clutter.
- ☐ Keep floors free of clutter.
- ☐ Keep desks and work spaces clear.
- ☐ Provide all materials needed for a task in the work space for that task.
- ☐ Donate or throw away unused and unnecessary items.
- ☐ Use pictures, symbols, or words to demonstrate task sequences.
- ☐ Offer checklists for homework, chores, and daily hygiene routines.
- ☐ Provide "chore logs" as a reminder and means of indicating when work is finished.
- ☐ Make color-coded entries on a calendar.
- ☐ Sort by "To Do" and "Done."
- ☐ Offer priority sorting for items to be done first, second, and so on.

▶ **Compensatory Strategies for Attention Deficits**

How effectively a child uses compensatory strategies is dependent on the relative integrity of two other processes—language and self-awareness—both of which provide the means for the child to internalize attentional control via self-generated cueing. Depending on the child's level of sophistication with language, compensatory strategies may need to be brief and simple so the demand on the child's language system is minimal and strategies become easy to remember. You can also use catch phrases and preparatory cues in therapy, but it is important to do so consistently before expecting the child to perform any given task.

As with any compensatory strategy, the child must understand the need for the strategy, must become aware of when to use it, and must be able to self-initiate the strategy. Knowledge of the child's self-regulatory capacities is necessary in order to determine if this approach to treatment has the potential for success.

> The most desirable outcome when teaching compensatory strategies would be for the child to internalize the compensatory strategies in order to use self-talk as a means of compensating for skill deficits.

The Source for Development of Executive Functions
Copyright © 2005 LinguiSystems, Inc.

Functional Strategies and Goals

If a child can learn what her strategies are and use them reliably and consistently, then improvement will be realized. Patience may be necessary more than anything else, since you will be the external source of compensation for quite some time. We have worked with children who took an entire academic year to learn three strategies, but once this information was internalized, they began to spontaneously use it in a variety of environments.

It is also important for the people who interact with the child to use the same compensatory strategies being taught in therapy. This consistency reinforces learning and promotes generalization to a variety of environments. It also provides the child with multiple opportunities to experience how a simple strategy may make a difference in her ability to communicate or work effectively. There is very little that anyone can do to impose the use of compensatory strategies if the child is unmotivated or uninterested in using the strategies. Being successful is the best internal motivator there is.

☑ **Quick list of compensatory strategies to promote attention:**

Things to Say
- ☐ "Get ready to listen."
- ☐ "I'm going to say something now."
- ☐ "Are you ready to watch?"
- ☐ "Turn off your hands/mouth."
- ☐ "Now you have to listen."
- ☐ "Time to work."

Things to Do
- ☐ Repeat information as needed.
- ☐ Restate information to provide multiple opportunities for processing.
- ☐ Confirm understanding before initiating activity.
- ☐ Request immediate recall and explanation of the information from the child.
- ☐ Use focused/attentive listening to facilitate processing.
- ☐ Use rehearsal to assist in retention of information.
- ☐ Use visualization techniques if the child is a visual learner.
- ☐ Use mnemonics.
- ☐ Chunk or categorize information.

Functional Strategies and Goals

▶ Sample Goals for Attention Deficits

- ✓ The child will demonstrate 80% accuracy for comprehension of two-part directions when given moderate verbal cues for attentive/focused listening.

- ✓ The child will follow one-step directions with 85% accuracy during functional tasks when given minimal verbal cues for focused attention.

- ✓ The child will recall and restate five related items in functional lists with 90% accuracy when given moderate verbal cues for attentive listening and use of compensatory strategies (repeat, rehearse, confirm).

- ✓ The child will independently use listening strategies (self-cue to listen, repeat and confirm information, request repetitions) to achieve auditory comprehension of short stories with 90% accuracy.

- ✓ The child will sustain attention for the duration of a simple homework sheet when given minimal verbal redirection in a nondistracting, structured environment.

- ✓ The child will demonstrate sufficient attention for completion of self-help skills (take a shower, brush teeth, get dressed) with moderate verbal cues to engage attention and independent use of visual cue cards placed in nondistracting environment.

- ✓ The child will demonstrate adequate shifting of attention between classroom teacher and classroom aide for following directions with 85% accuracy when given independent use of compensatory strategies (tell self who is talking, listen, repeat and confirm directions).

- ✓ The child will demonstrate attention to relevant input in social situations for appropriate understanding of nonverbal cues.

- ✓ The child will demonstrate sufficient attention, listening, and working memory to comprehend and retain simple short stories with 80% accuracy when given decreased rate of information and repetitions as needed.

- ✓ The child will demonstrate sustained attention for simple, single visual tasks sufficient to achieve 90% accuracy over a time period of 5 minutes with no distractions.

Functional Strategies and Goals

▶ Teaching Specific Attention Skills

In addition to highlighting self-awareness, minimizing potential distractions in the environment, and teaching compensatory strategies, you may also want to directly address development of attention as a skill set. Improved language performance or adaptive behavior may depend upon improving focused attention, the duration of attention, the division of attention, or the rapid shifting of attention. Teaching this specific skill may require more time in therapy, and the child may present with more functional and immediate needs than improved attention. If that is the case, then the previous sections for modifying the environment or introducing compensatory strategies would be the most efficient way to address attention issues. However, if time and opportunity allow, exercises designed to drill attention may be appropriate.

One general principle for treatment is to select activities that are completed easily by the child, so that cognitive efforts are diverted to maintaining the quality and time of attention to task. The focus must always be on accuracy for the given tasks (which assumes vigilance for errors in work) and maintaining this quality of work for increasing amounts of time. Behavioral charts and rewards may be useful during these types of treatment activities to provide the child with visual representations of her success.

☑ Quick list of sample tasks to increase attention and memory:
- ☐ Visual scanning tasks (rows of letters, numbers, symbols on a page; child is given a target to cross out every time it occurs on the page)
- ☐ Selective listening tasks (similar to visual scanning except information presented verbally and the child is required to signify when the target is heard)
- ☐ Listen and repeat lists of words. Start with 2-3 and increase to 5-7 words.
- ☐ Listen and repeat sentences, messages, descriptions. Start with brief single sentences and increase content and length.
- ☐ Present directions for the child to follow. Start with one-step related commands, increase to three-step related commands, and then to unrelated directions.
- ☐ Present a task in a controlled environment with minimal distractions. Gradually introduce planned distractions (e.g., background noise) and increase complexity of the task.

Functional Strategies and Goals

Impulsivity/Poor Inhibition

There is a distinct difference between the perception that a child is a deliberate risk-taker, and understanding that a child is unable to regulate the impulse to act or speak before thinking. The capacity to inhibit one's behaviors until a more appropriate time, or until a more appropriate set of behaviors can be determined, is not automatic. Nor is the lack of inhibition necessarily a willful intention to behave in a destructive or disruptive manner. The ability to inhibit impulses is closely related to the capacity to regulate one's behavior. Specifically, *inhibition* is the ability to exert deliberate control over initial reactions, emotional impulses, planning, or self-focused needs.

- **Inhibition requires self-control.** Self-control is a component of the overall self-regulatory system. A child cannot exert control over behaviors and interactions unless there is awareness of self, the environment, and how the combination of interactions between those two entities can be modified and controlled. Although not always the case, children who are impulsive also tend to have reduced self-awareness and an overall deficit in self-regulation.

- **Impulsivity is also somewhat dependent and interactive with attention.** Attention to a task or conversation is necessary for a child to recognize environmental cues and prompts that help identify the need for a more appropriate course of action. Impulsive actions may simply reflect a lack of knowledge about current task demands, resulting in the unplanned and impulsive use of previously learned response sets. Once attention to the environment is focused, it must also be sustained long enough to delay initial response patterns while other plans are made. Children who present with ADD/ADHD or other diagnoses with a component of inattention may fall into this category of impulsivity.

- **Impulsivity may also reflect an inability to actually determine an appropriate plan of action.** Attention may be intact; self awareness may be functional; but the ability to deliberately identify the necessary strategy, steps, and support systems needed for a given interaction may be lacking. As a result, the child impulsively resorts to previously learned response sets to substitute for her inability to coordinate a better plan. Children who lack the language necessary to plan abstractions or predict outcomes may demonstrate impulsive behaviors, seemingly unaware of the impact of their actions on the environment around them.

The Source for Development of Executive Functions

Functional Strategies and Goals

- **Impulsivity can also be seen in children who present with social inflexibility or rigid internal needs that are not in sync with external environmental expectations.** These children may be skilled at predicting outcomes or planning deliberate courses of action; however, their poor tolerance and comfort level for altering patterns of behavior limit the variety of responses they can demonstrate. Such emotionally-driven internal need for sameness in activities and conversation may be seen as impulsive as the child attempts to drive the interaction to meet her own needs.

Working with impulsivity requires patience, consistency, and the ability to tolerate expressions of frustration. The main focus of therapy must be a blend of functional outcomes (communicative and/or behavioral) for the environments in which the impulsivity is most problematic or observed. A combination of approaches is generally the most successful, depending upon the level of language and awareness that the child possesses.

▶ Environmental Modifications for Impulsivity/Poor Inhibition

Impulsive children often require extensive external supervision, if for no other reason than to keep them safe. Smaller children who have not yet developed the capacity for impulse control normally require safety controls within the environment, such as plastic electrical outlet covers, safety gates on stairways, locked cabinets, etc. These are changes we make to the environment as a matter of course, expecting to impose similar barriers for as long as the child requires. As internal impulse control and inhibition develop, we expect to make less invasive structural changes to our environment. We begin to change over to using verbal directives as a means of prompting and teaching the development of internal inhibition and self-control.

For the child who fails to develop these internal mechanisms to inhibit behaviors, which range from dangerous to simply embarrassing, we can make immediate changes in a child's appropriateness and safety by considering the surrounding environment. Limiting exposure to tempting, intrusive, and irrelevant items can often allow a child to redirect her attention and processing to more relevant and useful input.

Functional Strategies and Goals

☑ **Quick list of environmental modifications to reduce impact of impulsivity/poor inhibition:**
  ☐ Keep potentially dangerous items out of reach and inaccessible to the child.
  ☐ Put away items that are not yet needed.
  ☐ Keep control of necessary materials with the adult.
  ☐ Remove items of particular interest to a child, providing only relevant and necessary materials.
  ☐ Remove distracting items.
  ☐ Put "stop" signs on doors.

In addition to these simple environmental changes, we can use behavioral techniques to reward the child's ability to work within this environment. Negative consequences can also be used to shape a child's compliance with situational expectations, whether in structured treatment settings or in naturalistic environments.

Examples of behavioral shaping to reduce impulsivity:

- Provide verbal praise for delayed action.

- Use negative consequences and withdraw rewards for impulsive behavior that exceeds rule boundaries.

- Use gestural cues to delay actions or words.

- Withhold necessary materials or information until the desired delay-time has been achieved.

- Patiently and calmly restate a direction until it can be completed.

▶ **Compensatory Strategies for Impulsivity/Poor Inhibition**

If a child has enough self-awareness to verbalize and identify moments of impulsive behavior or communication, she may have the capacity to learn to use compensatory strategies to alter her behavior. Increasing a child's awareness of impulsivity often requires immediate feedback as soon as a negative consequence of the impulsive behavior occurs. Because these children often act or speak so quickly, there may not be much time to analyze or plan a response to the behavior; however, the overall intent of imposing or teaching compensatory strategies is to introduce a delay prior to actions.

The Source for Development of Executive Functions
Copyright © 2005 LinguiSystems, Inc.

Functional Strategies and Goals

☑ **Quick list of compensatory strategies and external cues to promote inhibition:**

Things to Say
- ☐ "What are you trying to accomplish?"
- ☐ "Let's write down what we're going to do before we start."
- ☐ "Do you have a plan?"
- ☐ "What are you going to do first?"
- ☐ "Let's write down the steps we're going to do."
- ☐ "Wait. We don't have a plan yet."
- ☐ "You're interrupting. Remember, we're practicing waiting."

Things to Do
- ☐ Keep items required for the task with you until the child verbalizes a coherent plan and intent.
- ☐ Use light physical contact (e.g., a touch to the shoulder) to remind the child to preplan before acting.
- ☐ Impose brief delays in responses (2-3 seconds) by using a hand gesture or stop sign to indicate a wait time.

Providing external cues in verbal or physical form may be the only way to impose inhibition during initial phases of treatment. At some point, however, it is desirable to teach the child to use self-talk strategies to begin to transition cueing from an external source to an internal, self-regulated source. Phrases need to be designed with the child's language system in mind, and often need to be repeated and rehearsed until they become internalized. Catch phrases can also be provided in simple, clear written form on index cards, chalkboards, whiteboards, or any other means that capture the child's attention.

☑ **Quick list of self-talk strategies to promote inhibition:**
- ☐ "I need to think first."
- ☐ "Stop, think, plan, do."
- ☐ "What's my plan?"
- ☐ "I need help."
- ☐ "Wait! What will happen if I do this?"
- ☐ "Count to 10."
- ☐ "It's not my turn yet."

Functional Strategies and Goals

▶ **Sample Goals for Impulsivity in Social Interactions**

✓ The child will limit interruptions in structured conversation with peers to less than four times per topic when given moderate-to-maximum verbal and gestural cues.

✓ The child will take turns in structured play situations for 80% of opportunities when given minimal verbal reminders to use self-talk cues.

✓ The child will use appropriate social greetings at the beginning and end of each session.

✓ The child will demonstrate preplanning for verbal responses in structured descriptive tasks, limiting sentence length to five words per object when given physical cues (hold up fingers to count each word given).

✓ The child will demonstrate preplanning for responses to questions by delaying a response for 10 seconds for 80% of trials when given a visual timer.

✓ The child will evaluate topic introduction as relevant/irrelevant with 85% accuracy when given written cue cards to prompt assessment.

✓ The child will demonstrate appropriate physical space and proximity to others in structured play settings when given moderate-to-maximum physical and verbal cues.

✓ The child will demonstrate expected behavior (e.g., no yelling, listen, nice hands, do our work) when given visual cues and one verbal warning per impulsive outburst.

▶ **Sample Goals for Impulsivity in Problem Solving**

✓ The child will state intent and first two steps to plan prior to initiating efforts for simple paper/pencil academic tasks 80% of the time when given moderate-to-maximum verbal cues.

✓ The child will independently delay efforts to solve novel problems for a 5-minute planning time with 75% accuracy.

✓ The child will use self-talk cues to state a planned, deliberate strategy for simple functional tasks 80% of the time with minimal verbal cues.

Functional Strategies and Goals

✓ The child will successfully complete self-help tasks (e.g., shower, dress) using environmental cue cards to delay actions until all necessary items are available.

✓ The child will successfully complete academic worksheets requiring reading and writing with 80% accuracy when given moderate-to-maximum cues to delay efforts until the entire page is visually scanned.

✓ The child will verbally state her plan prior to initiating efforts for 80% of simple problem-solving activities when given minimal verbal reminders to use self-talk cues.

✓ The child will demonstrate attentive listening to instructions and restate them with 90% accuracy prior to receiving materials to complete a task when given repetition as necessary.

Impaired Self-Awareness and Self-Monitoring

Chapter 5 discussed the importance of establishing self-awareness, self-monitoring, and self-adaptation within a metacognitive framework. Therapy plans must work to advance the level of self-awareness first, so that goals for self-correction and improved adaptive behavior can be established.

A child's ability to generalize across environments and function as independently as possible is inherently connected to the capacity to acquire self-awareness and self-monitoring. It would be beneficial to take a closer look at children who struggle to communicate or apply language skills they have demonstrated in isolated contexts. Deficits in self-awareness and self-monitoring can cause inconsistent application or use of intact executive function and language skills. This results in ineffective problem solving as well as social or pragmatic breakdowns. Addressing the executive function skills of self-awareness and self-monitoring are more likely to result in improved application of acquired language skills.

> Consider a case in which the child presented with abrupt, impulsive, interruptive, and inattentive social interaction. Both peers and the adults in this child's life acknowledged frustration with her off-topic responses, rule-breaking in board games, inappropriately verbose responses, and inability to remember instructions or requests.

Functional Strategies and Goals

Before beginning to improve attention, pragmatic skills, and inhibition, goals to promote self-awareness were implemented. Videotapes of the child's interactions were used in therapy to provide firsthand evidence of the identified deficits. Goals were written that required the child to demonstrate awareness of the deficits. Initially, the clinician identified moments of socially inappropriate behaviors when they occurred on videotape. The clinician also used the technique of demonstrating the observed behaviors, prompting the child to begin evaluating the clinician's rule-breaking and interruptive comments.

Gradually the child developed the ability to identify pragmatic social errors independently. Goals were then advanced to incorporate teaching compensatory strategies designed to overcome the deficits. The child's future goals focused on transitioning the responsibility for self-monitoring and correcting from an external source to an internalized system. The ultimate objective was to improve the overall quality of behavioral interactions.

☑ **Quick list of techniques to promote developing awareness, monitoring, and self-correction:**
- ☐ Provide immediate, specific, direct feedback the moment inappropriate social interactions or ineffective efforts occur.
- ☐ Video- and audiotape undesired behaviors for objective concrete viewing.
- ☐ Chart inappropriate social interactions.
- ☐ Use a diary to record deficits and goal implementation.
- ☐ Use charts or graphs to track performance.
- ☐ Practice identifying ineffective problem solving in others.
- ☐ Compare the child's predicted accuracy levels with actual accuracy levels.
- ☐ Use role playing and group interactions to promote awareness.
- ☐ Use planned failure tasks to force identification of errors.
- ☐ Begin work on self-correction/use of strategies in structured, nondistracting environments.
- ☐ Transition to self-correction and self-driven adaptation in less-structured environments with planned distractions.
- ☐ Generalize to unpredictable and distracting environments.

Functional Strategies and Goals

▶ **Sample Goals for Establishing Awareness of Deficits**

✓ The child will state two (three, four, etc.) reasons for attending speech therapy when given visual cues, discussion, or examples, as needed.

✓ The child will independently explain two goals of speech therapy at the beginning and end of each session.

✓ The child will identify specific examples of perseverative problem-solving efforts for 80% of occurrences when given videotape review of previous sessions and moderate-to-maximum verbal cues.

✓ The child will acknowledge off-topic comments and irrelevant responses when given immediate, specific verbal feedback from a clinician 80% of the time.

✓ The child will identify specific examples of communication breakdowns for 80% of occurrences with minimal prompting.

✓ The child will identify examples of socially inappropriate communication with maximum verbal cues, use of video/audiotaped examples, and direct/immediate verbal feedback.

✓ The child will demonstrate increased awareness of the need for help when given moderate verbal cues for 70% of opportunities.

✓ The child will identify examples of conversational interruptions for 75% of instances when given visual feedback (e.g., viewing a videotape of self in conversation).

✓ The child will identify instances of problem-solving breakdown four times per functional task when given maximum verbal cues.

✓ The child will explain need for environmental cue cards listing each step and sequence for completing a task (e.g., taking a shower).

▶ **Sample Goals for Establishing Awareness of Compensatory Strategies**

✓ In each session, the child will state three compensatory strategies for effective problem solving when given maximum verbal review, use of visual lists, and immediate feedback during functional problem-solving activities.

Functional Strategies and Goals

- ✓ The child will independently state two compensatory strategies for effective sequencing of plans (e.g., make lists of necessary materials, use visual cue cards for 1st, 2nd, 3rd, etc.).

- ✓ The child will demonstrate independent use of compensatory strategies for impulsivity in functional task completion. Examples of self-talk to accomplish this goal include the following: "Stop, think, plan, do" "What is my plan?" and "I'll work slowly to get them all right."

- ✓ The child will verbally explain two out of three compensatory strategies to peers in a social group when given minimal reminders and examples.

- ✓ The child will independently explain three compensatory strategies to her classroom teacher with sufficient examples.

- ✓ The child will independently demonstrate use of three compensatory strategies to her parents in a structured clinical setting with no distractions during a functional practice situation.

▶ **Sample Goals for Increasing Self-Monitoring and Evaluation**

- ✓ The child's predicted outcomes for functional tasks/problem solving will match actual outcomes with 80% accuracy when given moderate amounts of visual cues (e.g., written evaluation) and verbal feedback.

- ✓ The child will identify 75% of all errors in work when given maximum cues for impulsivity and concepts of cause/effect.

- ✓ The child will monitor her own behavior and execution skills with 80% accuracy when given minimal external input during functional outings in unstructured environments.

- ✓ The child will identify 80% of all errors in completed work when given moderate-to-maximum verbal cues and use of examples in nondistracting, controlled environments.

- ✓ The child will independently identify 85% of all errors in task execution.

- ✓ The child will execute a sequence of steps to complete a simple task with 90% accuracy when given maximum verbal cues to identify errors in work.

Functional Strategies and Goals

▶ **Sample Goals for Self-Correction**

✓ The child will execute a sequence of steps to complete a plan with 90% accuracy, stopping to self-correct as needed, when given minimal cues to identify errors.

✓ The child will demonstrate use of compensatory strategies for problem solving (e.g., evaluate each step for success, request help when stuck) during 75% of opportunities when given minimal reminders and prompts.

✓ The child will independently refer to external cues (e.g., lists, signs, reminders, calendars) for 85% of opportunities to verbally convey accurate information when errors are identified by the clinician.

✓ The child will refer to external cues (e.g., lists, signs, reminders, calendars) for 70% of opportunities to verbally convey accurate information when independently identifying factual errors.

✓ The child will increase intelligibility during functional communication activities by independently using compensatory strategies (e.g., slow rate of speech, repeat message) for 75% of opportunities.

✓ The child will self-correct errors in simple problem-solving tasks 80% of the time after errors are identified by the clinician.

✓ The child will self-cue to reread skipped lines on homework papers 75% of the time in a nondistracting environment.

✓ The child will demonstrate use of conversational repair strategies when needed during unstructured social interactions when given minimal reminders.

✓ The child will use compensatory strategies (e.g., double-check work, use check marks to indicate items completed), given maximum verbal cues and reminders, to achieve 80% accuracy for reading comprehension and written expression in academic paper-pencil tasks in a controlled environment.

✓ The child will independently use compensatory strategies (e.g., double-check work, use check marks to indicate items completed, use blank paper to cover up work not in use, use a ruler as line guide, restate desired outcome of a task, seek minimally distracting work space) to achieve 90% accuracy for reading comprehension and written expression in academic paper-pencil tasks.

Functional Strategies and Goals

Deficits in Flexibility

Children who demonstrate rigidity in their performance may have significant difficulty generating novel or creative strategies to solve problems, even after failing. They may perseverate on unsuccessful or pointless approaches to problems, resulting in the need for significant amounts of external cueing and prompts. This inability to generate and modify strategies to meet the demands of a given situation ultimately limits independence and self-sufficiency.

In social situations, children with deficits in behavioral flexibility tend to resist unpredictability and the slightest change in their environment or routine. Events that may seem inconsequential to others may violate a child's threshold for sensory stimuli, impose stressful unpredictability, or require uncomfortable adaptation to others' needs and perspectives. These externally imposed demands for internal flexibility can contribute to anxiety or temperamental meltdowns for the child who needs "sameness." For example, many children with Asperger's syndrome exhibit intense personal interests that tend to dominate interactions with other students. The resulting social behavior is often inappropriate or insensitive. Communication interactions lack transitions and the give-and-take pragmatic exchanges expected in play or conversation.

> Tyler was an 8-year-old boy with a working diagnosis of nonverbal learning disorder with tendencies toward Asperger's syndrome. His parents expressed concern over Tyler's intense level of anxiety in daily life. As conversations with the parents ensued, a picture of Tyler's inflexibility in daily routines became apparent. He could not get ready for school without asking his mother repeatedly whether or not his regular teacher would be there. On other occasions, he asked the same questions over and over again, almost nonstop, about what time they would leave for the store, what were they going to buy, and whether he might hear loud noises there. A near constant stream of reassurance was necessary to give Tyler the capacity to carry on with his day.
>
> Tyler's tolerance for unpredictable or novel situations was nearly incapacitating. After attending an initial group therapy session with three other children who also had social and pragmatic impairments, Tyler collapsed on the floor in tears. He was unable to express his feelings about the interaction until several days later, when he verbalized frustration and anxiety about the loudness of one child's voice, the erratic physical movements of another child, and the uncertainty of a new routine. Tyler's parents and the SLP agreed that the pressure of having to modify his own internal needs were better suited to individual therapy sessions. Tyler's treatment goals focused on improving his ability to verbalize anxiety, learning compensatory strategies for managing social interactions, and practicing structured and planned interactions with a familiar communication partner before moving back into a group dynamic.

Functional Strategies and Goals

In general, the world around us rarely meets our own individual, internal routines; we are required to adjust. Flexibility as a component of normally developing executive functions means that a child can create new strategies to solve problems when others have failed. It means a child can make adjustments in performance as necessary and modify social interactions to reflect sensitivity to others' needs and interests. The inability to adapt can result not only in pragmatic impairments, but also decreased self-sufficiency, limited independence, and anxiety.

Other forms of inflexibility appear as deficits in problem solving and thinking.

Stephen was a 13-year-old boy with autism who functioned well in several regular education classes and had fairly good verbal communication skills. Goals focused mainly on promoting self-sufficiency for simple self-care tasks, household chores, and novel problem solving to begin transitioning to better adaptive life skills. Stephen's ability to generate multiple plans and strategies was fairly good; however, the presence of certain rigid needs occasionally limited how effectively he was able to implement the generated ideas.

One project for Stephen was to figure out how to make an hourglass that would run through in a specified amount of time. Stephen and his therapy partner were given two empty water bottles, some tape, and various dried materials, such as sugar, rice, and beans. The boys' plans were generally good; however, Stephen's focus on the amount of tape required, the placement of the tape, and the need for only him to secure the tape rather than his partner, significantly extended the amount of time required to finish the project (two hours!). In addition, Stephen's focus on retaping the bottles in a certain manner each time interfered with their memory for which dried material had just been tried. The boys used rice over and over again, instead of moving on to a different option.

☑ **Quick list of techniques to promote flexibility in problem solving:**
- ☐ Verbal fluency—name as many items in a category as possible
- ☐ Design fluency—make as many creations as possible using Legos, Ellos, blocks, etc.
- ☐ Situational problem-solving tasks—generate as many solutions as possible (e.g., "What would you do if . . . ?")
- ☐ Simple science experiments, no-bake cooking tasks, simulated or real household chores
- ☐ Limiting availability of one or more required items for a task

Functional Strategies and Goals

▶ Sample Goals for Increasing Flexibility in Problem Solving

✓ The child will generate four potential strategies for simple problem-solving tasks when given maximum verbal cues to predict the outcome of each strategy.

✓ The child will develop two viable strategies for homework completion when given maximum verbal cues to predict outcomes for each strategy.

✓ The child will predict the outcome of each potential strategy with 85% accuracy when given moderate-to-maximum verbal feedback and use of written notes to focus efforts.

✓ The child will independently select the best strategy for problem-solving tasks when given current situational demands for 75% of opportunities.

✓ The child will identify failed strategies 80% of the time when given maximum verbal cues to compare results with intent for household chores requiring reading and listening comprehension for instructions.

✓ The child will independently create and apply strategies until a problem is solved 85% of the time.

✓ The child will state four different uses of common household items when given moderate verbal cues.

✓ The child will improvise use of available materials to complete academic projects within a given time frame with moderate-to-maximum cues to generate alternative ideas.

✓ The child will demonstrate sufficient reading and listening comprehension to complete errands with minimal cues for implied or incomplete information.

Functional Strategies and Goals

☑ **Quick list of techniques to promote flexibility in social situations:**
  ☐ Teach specific skills in structured environments.
  ☐ Transition to role-playing interactions.
  ☐ Work with materials or topics of interest before applying skills to situations the child dislikes or is uninterested in.
  ☐ Provide planned and predictable transitions before unexpected transitions.
  ☐ Add planned distractions before unplanned distractions.
  ☐ Graduate to uncontrolled and unpredictable environments.
  ☐ Evaluate the child's capacity to correctly read social cues requiring some adaptation in behavior.

▶ **Sample Goals for Increasing Flexibility in Social Situations**

✓ The child will use appropriate requests, as opposed to taking items of interest, during 90% of opportunities with minimal verbal cues during structured play situations.

✓ The child will take turns with 90% accuracy, without verbal cues from the clinician, during structured conversations on topics of interest to the child.

✓ The child will spontaneously use appropriate turn-taking skills during play-based interactions using toys of high-interest.

✓ The child will follow behavior rules of therapy (e.g., no yelling, listen, nice hands, do your work) when given one verbal warning before moving from "green" to "yellow" and losing the privilege.

✓ The child will modify and use appropriate vocal intensity in therapy 80% of the time when given moderate verbal and gestural cues, such as hands over ears or exaggerated facial expressions.

✓ The child will demonstrate successful, nondisruptive transitions between activities when given a written or visual plan and minimal verbal cues.

✓ The child will demonstrate successful, nondisruptive social interaction for unexpected transitions to unknown tasks 80% of the time when given maximum verbal direction.

✓ The child will use appropriate language to identify and express emotions during stressful interactions 75% of the time when given direct prompting and closed-ended questions.

Functional Strategies and Goals

Deficits in Goal Selection

As a component of executive functions, goal selection implies the ability to determine a course of action that is in keeping with one's long-term plans or the requirements of a social group. It is the ability to make a link between what a person is doing now and how this action will affect what is experienced later. Younger children require guidance from their parents and teachers in this area because they are not yet able to delay gratification for immediate desires to receive a future reward. As frontal lobe development occurs in conjunction with the acquisition of more abstract language and syntax, children begin to make connections between "if . . . then" statements and to impose delays in behavior for later rewards. They begin to see the basis for what they judge to be "wise" choices.

Children who have deficits in determining goals may have difficulty identifying a course of action for simple things that are expected for their age level, such as deciding not to leave their bikes outside or prioritizing the day's homework. They may be unable to focus their efforts on one particular activity and may end up wasting time on what we perceive to be irrelevant, scattered, or destructive activity. Children may have difficulty identifying exactly what to do, as well as how to do it. They appear to be at a loss for how to follow the direction to "clean up your room," even if they are motivated to do so and want to please the parent.

Other children may demonstrate poor goal selection of a more serious nature, resulting in more significant consequences. These children may have trouble taking the perspective of others, don't experience empathy for other's situations, or can't identify potential problems. As these children grow and are given more freedom to independently weigh options and potential outcomes, they make choices that can negatively impact not only themselves, but others.

As with any other deficit executive function skill, the inability to identify a goal, whether simple or complex, immediate or long-term, may exist in combination with other deficits. The capacity to use language to prioritize and identify relevant cues may be impaired. The child may only select one aspect of the big picture to work on, without clearly identifying the global requirements of a task or interaction. Perhaps the child is able to identify a need for action and develop the necessary strategic plans, but must be prompted to do so.

Functional Strategies and Goals

Consider the child who was attempting to purchase a snack for himself (a drink and chips) and found his way to the snack bar. For this particular child, the abstraction of thought required to make the connection between "soda" and "drinks," and "snacks" and "candy bar" proved to be too complex a link to make. The child was unable to determine what to do (enter the snack shop and make his purchase), despite being given maximum verbal cues designed to promote making this link independently. The clinician had to provide multiple verbal prompts to continue clarifying and making the link externally. "Can you buy a drink here? Can you buy soda here? Do you see candy bars on the shelf? What should we do?" In addition, this child demonstrated a complete shut down of physical and verbal activity. He was not only unable to respond to these cues, he was also unable to initiate walking into the doorway of the shop, and he could not make eye contact with the therapist. He was literally at a complete stand-still, overwhelmed with input and unable to identify a goal.

For this child, the only way he was able to determine a goal for himself was after being given specific and direct verbal cues: "This store has soda and candy bars. You can buy the ones you want here. We need to go in now." The child's language deficit, combined with an inability to initiate any form of action, resulted in deficit goal selection. After being told "We need to go in now," the child still required physical prompts to initiate walking toward the entrance of the shop. Once inside, he was able to independently identify and execute the necessary steps to find and purchase the desired items on his own.

☑ **Quick list of techniques to promote goal selection:**
- ☐ Compare and contrast exercises
- ☐ Interpretation of If . . . then statements
- ☐ Deductive/conclusive reasoning tasks
- ☐ Using hypothetical situations to foster predictions
- ☐ Promoting the ability to make inferences
- ☐ Using written lists of prediction outcomes to support memory and comparison
- ☐ Promoting the ability to select advantageous versus destructive plans

▶ **Sample Goals for Increasing Goal Identification/Problem Recognition**

✓ The child will identify and state the presence of a problem with 80% accuracy when experiencing various functional situations.

✓ The child will state the most relevant and appropriate solution to problems with 80% accuracy when given no verbal cues.

Functional Strategies and Goals

- ✓ The child will identify situations leading to problems with 75% accuracy when given visual context and input.

- ✓ The child will identify and state the presence of a problem with 75% accuracy when given visual context/line drawings of situations.

- ✓ The child will generate alternate solutions to problems, when necessary, with 75% accuracy when given maximum verbal cueing and analytical support.

- ✓ The child will generate as many possible solutions to problems as possible when given minimal cues to remain on task.

- ✓ The child will select the most relevant and useful solution when provided with independent analysis of a problem.

- ✓ The child will select two potential solutions when given maximum cues for relevance and comparison to task requirements.

- ✓ The child will state intentions using simple, specific sentences when given maximum verbal cues to attend to environmental cues, such as signs, notices, and menus.

- ✓ The child will develop and explain one strategy to complete an assigned homework chore with consideration for time constraints when given moderate cues for predicting the potential effectiveness of the strategy to meet task requirements.

Impaired Initiation

Deficits in the ability to initiate deliberate, goal-oriented efforts can be a frustration to the child, teacher, and parent. Behaviors can include a child who shuts down physically or verbally, evidenced by prolonged silence or outbursts of frustration. Some children are unable to provide an explanation for their frustration. As a result, the parent or professional has no idea why the child is unable to complete a seemingly simple and well-explained task.

Functional Strategies and Goals

Parents often complain that they need to constantly nag a child if they want something to get done, particularly if time constraints are involved. The child may be described as being lazy or unmotivated, when the problem is actually very different. Providing education, information, and counseling is appropriate in these instances. If a parent or teacher can observe an example of how external cues can promote the initiation of planned intentions, they are usually very willing to provide them to the child.

Matthew, the 14-year-old boy described in the assessment case studies, was typically unable to initiate a task when he became overwhelmed by demands that exceeded his threshold for length and complexity of linguistic and executive function processing. It required several sessions of observing Matthew before it became apparent that he was not trying to avoid completing a task or responding to a question. Instead, Matthew's silence, head held down in his hands, and lack of eye contact were all signs of his inability to initiate both physical and verbal movement. The SLP had to literally use gentle physical strength to pull Matthew's hands down from his face, lift up his chin, and request eye contact.

At that point, Matthew was given specific verb phrases to direct his efforts, starting with "stand up." This was combined with gentle but firm physical guidance, with a hand placed on Matthew's elbow as he walked, to lead him to the counter where he was to prepare a no-bake snack for himself. The task instructions were written in simple, clear language. He had been provided with all the necessary utensils and ingredients. However, once at the counter, he again withdrew into his closed, "shutdown" mode. Verbal and physical cues were again required to help Matthew initiate efforts.

Hand-over-hand assistance was used to help Matthew crush cookies with a rolling pin until he could sustain this movement independently. Closed-ended questions were addressed to Matthew while he completed the motions. As Matthew began to be able to respond to yes/no questions, the clinician transitioned to forced-choice questions, followed by specific, open-ended questions. Initially, Matthew could not independently sustain efforts to continue with both the physical and the verbal activities simultaneously. He could either crush cookies silently or talk excessively without crushing cookies. Over the course of the next 10 minutes, nearly all physical cues were faded to a single touch on the arm and the use of the verbal prompt, "and then what?" Matthew's ability to initiate and maintain physical and verbal activities improved, and he was able to successfully make his snack in a timely fashion.

The lists on pages 163-164 offer suggestions to promote initiation via external or environmental cues. These are especially helpful for the child who experiences significant impairments in initiation, either for verbal expression or physical activity, directed toward a functional goal.

Functional Strategies and Goals

☑ **Quick list of external cues to promote initiation:**
  ☐ Offer physical cues to help initiate motor movement.
  ☐ Create, laminate, and hang simple step-by-step lists for daily self-care tasks.
  ☐ Post laminated reminders in key places.
  ☐ Pair physical activity with verbal expression.
  ☐ Use music and rhythm to promote expression and movement.
  ☐ Use visual or picture cues to promote initiation of expressive language.

☑ **Quick list of environmental modifications and tasks to promote initiation:**
  ☐ Divide tasks into smaller, more obvious steps.
  ☐ Use organizational systems to remind/prompt.
  ☐ Give first starting steps, in addition to subtask direction.
  ☐ Use checklists to transition from "To Do" to "Done."
  ☐ Use "go" signs to prompt continued efforts between steps.
  ☐ Use timers or time constraints to prompt efforts.
  ☐ Turn chores into "contests" to see how quickly or accurately they can be done.

As SLPs, we can also foster initiation as a skill and reduce children's frustration by altering the way in which we communicate. Some key points for modifying our own language to assist these children are listed below.

☑ **Quick list of language modifications to promote initiation:**
  ☐ Use specific, concrete language.
  ☐ Use verb phrases.
  ☐ Ask *yes/no* questions.
  ☐ Do not assume comprehension of implied instructions.
  ☐ Give step-by-step instructions, rather than global instructions.
  ☐ Give forced choices for initial steps of the task, such as "Fold first or sort first."
  ☐ Use simple verb phrases instead of lengthy instructions, such as "Stand here" or "Look up."
  ☐ Ask if the child knows what she wants to say or do.
  ☐ Ask the child if she needs help getting started.
  ☐ Direct the child to make eye contact.
  ☐ Offer verbal praise for completion of parts of a bigger task.

The Source for Development of Executive Functions
Copyright © 2005 LinguiSystems, Inc.

Functional Strategies and Goals

To gain self-sufficiency, a child's need for external cues or environmental modifications for initiation must be decreased. Teaching children how to request assistance can be one of the single most useful compensatory strategies to offer. Simply asking for help, although this seems to be a fairly obvious strategy, may not be simple or self-evident to the child who cannot internally organize and initiate effort. The lack of a verbal request for assistance, such as "I don't know how" or "Help me start," can be perplexing for family members and teachers, especially when the child may have already stated her intentions or can verbally repeat the task expectations.

☑ **Quick list of self-cued compensatory strategies to promote initiation:**
- ☐ "I need help."
- ☐ "Please, say it again."
- ☐ "I need more time to think."
- ☐ "Give me a choice."
- ☐ "Help me get started."
- ☐ "Do it with me first."

▶ **Sample Goals for Initiation**

✓ The child will generate and initiate a response 70% of the time when given two choices for the next steps.

✓ The child will request help using self-talk strategies 80% of the time when given minimal verbal reminders.

✓ The child will initiate the use of verbal communication to express thoughts and responses (rather than physical outbursts) 75% of the time when given environmental and verbal modifications as needed.

✓ The child will independently initiate use of compensatory strategies to request help for 70% of opportunities when help is needed.

✓ The child will initiate the use of communication repair strategies for 80% of opportunities needed when given minimal verbal prompts.

✓ The child will retell four events of the day using a daily planner as an external cueing system.

Functional Strategies and Goals

- ✓ The child will demonstrate sufficient initiation and persistence to complete functional activities 80% of the time when given environmental cue cards and minimal verbal prompts.

- ✓ The child will initiate conversational topics during structured social exchanges when given moderate-to-maximum verbal cues.

- ✓ The child will respond appropriately when given two choices in instances of being unable to self-initiate a next step during 70% of opportunities.

- ✓ The child will complete self-help tasks 80% of the time with the use of external cue cards, minimal verbal prompts, and a timer.

Deficits in Perception and Expression of Social and Environmental Cues

These skills are necessary in order to select and initiate socially appropriate behavior, while meeting academic and vocational expectations, and to enjoy rewarding personal relationships.

Many children with deficits in executive functions demonstrate an inability to perceive nonverbal, social-emotional cues from the environment and people around them. Failure to recognize the implied meaning of facial expressions, prosody, body language, or inferred language can interfere with the process of selecting appropriate behavior in a given situation. Communication attempts may be off-topic or irrelevant. Behavior may not match the expectations of the environment, even when the conversational partner provides a rather obvious facial expression (e.g., as if to say "*What* are you talking about?").

> Being able to identify social and environmental cues impacts a wide variety of adaptive skills, such as the ability to form accurate impressions and opinions, identify implied or direct needs to alter a behavior in response to evolving situational demands, recognize potential and actual problems or disagreements, and understand others' feelings and needs.

Parents of children who struggle to comprehend social cues complain that the only way their child understands is when they say it simply, directly, and without ambiguity. Saying "It's time to go" with an exasperated facial expression is not likely to result in the child's getting up off the couch. These children require overly-obvious language and direct instruction, such as "Get off the couch. Turn off the TV. Walk to the back door with me. Put on your shoes. Let's go outside. Get inside the car now." The need to break down tasks into subparts is expected when a child is four years old, but not when the child is fourteen.

Functional Strategies and Goals

The use of intonation to convey frustration is typically lost on these children, as is the emotional subtext of an angry facial expression. The deficits in this area of executive functions contribute to an inability to take on the perspective of others. This might be evidenced by a rather perplexing behavior of seeming to be uninterested or unaffected by the problems of others—even when they have contributed to or directly caused the problem.

- ☑ **Quick list of techniques to promote social/environmental perception:**
    - ☐ Practice determining which social cues are relevant versus irrelevant.
    - ☐ Increase ability to draw conclusions from relevant social cues.
    - ☐ Work on understanding the "big picture."
    - ☐ Teach the skill of reading facial expressions, and provide vocabulary to match.
    - ☐ Teach the skill of reading body language, and provide vocabulary to match.
    - ☐ Improve the ability to interpret statements based on prosody.
    - ☐ Use a digital camera to document facial expressions for later discussion.
    - ☐ Promote development of emotional concepts via the use of scrapbooks for situations, facial expressions, and implied meanings.
    - ☐ Offer concept and vocabulary units on emotions, feelings, and social skills.

In addition to poor receptive understanding of social-emotional cues, children also demonstrate deficits in expressing social-emotional responses. These children are unable to internally modulate emotions into socially acceptable interactions. Impulsive behavioral responses occur, particularly for children who have limited self-regulatory skills. The children are often described as lacking empathy for others, including family members for whom the child has genuine love and affection.

A child with deficits in social expression might also try to dominate conversation and interactions. The social sense of "fairness" and order tend to be overlooked and replaced with internally-governed rules based on the child's own needs and interests. The child may feel a compelling need to win at every game—even to the point of blatantly cheating. Conversations may become reduced to one-sided dissertations, complete with yelling and interruptions in order for the child to maintain control. Simple transitions may become a battle of wills, with the adult often expressing daily exasperation at having tried every discipline technique under the sun with little change in the child's behavior.

Functional Strategies and Goals

☑ **Quick list of techniques to promote appropriate social communication and behavior:**
- ☐ Use a videotape to promote identification of inappropriate actions and verbalizations.
- ☐ Choose and enforce two or three fundamental expectations for behavior.
- ☐ Use negative consequences consistently.
- ☐ Use social skills stories to provide opportunities for discussion.
- ☐ Use role playing to provide opportunities for practice.
- ☐ Use direct language to cue behavior; "polite" language may be too obscure.
- ☐ Create circumstances to simulate emotional responses, such as "How would you feel if . . .".
- ☐ Provide direct, forced choices for action.
- ☐ Use pragmatic therapy and social skills training concepts.
- ☐ Use puppets as a means of practicing skills indirectly.

▶ **Sample Goals for Perception of Social, Nonverbal, and Environmental Cues**

✓ The child will verbalize accurate perceptions of appropriate versus inappropriate language in given social contexts.

✓ The child will demonstrate awareness of other's feelings or reactions to her behaviors for 75% of opportunities when given moderate verbal feedback paired with videotaped examples of others interacting with the child.

✓ The child will label and explain her own feelings from the day when given visual feedback (e.g., digital pictures of herself that day) and moderate verbal cues (e.g., choices, direct questions).

✓ The child will identify two nonverbal characteristics that identify how a person feels with 70% accuracy.

✓ The child will imitate sample intonation patterns of verbal statements with 80% accuracy when given auditory and visual feedback.

✓ The child will produce requested intonation patterns, such as questioning, angry, sad, curious, etc., with 80% accuracy when given minimal verbal feedback.

Functional Strategies and Goals

- ✓ The child will identify which cues in a pictured scene are relevant to the "title" of the picture with 80% accuracy when given minimal verbal feedback for inferences and deductive reasoning.

- ✓ The child will state the main idea of a social scene (via pictures, movie or TV clips, cartoons, etc.) with 80% accuracy when given minimal cues to identify relevant cues.

- ✓ The child will identify what makes a circumstance a "problem" with 80% accuracy when given maximum verbal cues and use of "How would *you* feel?" scenarios.

- ✓ The child will explain why a circumstance is problematic to those involved for 80% of opportunities when given minimal verbal prompts or choices.

▶ **Sample Goals for Developing Appropriate Social Communication and Behavior**

- ✓ The child will demonstrate appropriate nonverbal interaction, including eye contact and body language, during 70% of opportunities when given moderate verbal and physical cues.

- ✓ The child will demonstrate eye contact 20 times during the course of a five-minute conversation when given use of a visual cue card.

- ✓ The child will modify inappropriate social interactions for 60% of opportunities when given maximum verbal redirection.

- ✓ The child will follow rules of social games with peers 85% of the time when given moderate amounts of verbal feedback and prompting to verbalize a more appropriate behavior.

- ✓ The child will accurately demonstrate facial expressions for corresponding feelings with 80% accuracy when given maximum amounts of visual feedback.

- ✓ The child will produce requested intonation with 80% accuracy when given pictures of facial expressions and verbal labels of emotions to convey.

- ✓ The child will demonstrate the ability to share with others during structured play for 80% of opportunities when given minimal cues and reminders.

Functional Strategies and Goals

✓ The child will identify her own behaviors and label them as "appropriate" or "inappropriate" with 80% accuracy when given review of videotaped interactions.

✓ The child will generate a list of more appropriate behaviors for observed videotaped interaction when given minimal verbal cueing.

✓ The child will independently verbalize understanding of the difference between a "quiet" situation and a "loud" situation (e.g., test time versus playground time).

✓ The child will demonstrate appropriate nonverbal interaction, including eye contact and body language, during 70% of opportunities when given moderate verbal and physical cues.

✓ The child will select appropriate behaviors for various circumstances with 90% accuracy when given three choices.

Case Study Treatment Plans

In the assessment chapter, several case studies were presented. A short synopsis of those cases is provided in this section; however, it might be beneficial to review them for more extensive information. A sample treatment plan for each of the cases has been added in this chapter, providing a snapshot of the types of goals that are typical with various disorders, as well as approach strategies.

▶ **Child with Executive Function Deficits Associated with Williams Syndrome** (including ADD/ADHD and cognitive impairment)

Background Information
Matthew was a 15-year-old boy with a moderate language delay and deficits in executive function skills associated with a clinical diagnosis of Williams syndrome. As part of the Williams syndrome profile, Matthew was also diagnosed with attention deficit hyperactivity disorder (ADHD) and mental retardation at a mild-moderate level (educable mental impairment (EMH/EMI). The hyperactivity and inattention contributed to deficits in communication, behavior, and self-regulation. His rate of speech was quite rapid, and Matthew had difficulty maintaining the topic of conversation.

Functional Strategies and Goals

Treatment goals had transitioned to almost exclusively targeting executive function skills in the following areas:

- Increasing self-awareness and self-regulation abilities
- Improving functional communication for social, academic, and prevocational skills

Table 6.1 Matthew's Treatment Protocol

Goal	Method	Results
Self-monitor behavior and execution skills with 80% accuracy	Targeted goal indirectly through anticipating outcomes and restating the objectives of each therapy session	Matthew demonstrated an increased ability to anticipate outcomes and was able to state the general therapy objectives of "Think better, look at people, and talk clearly." He was also able to report "thinking better" with successful completion of a task.
Increase awareness of the need for help when given moderate verbal cues during 70% of opportunities	Providing frequent verbal cues to prompt Matthew to ask for help	Although initially unaware of his need for help, Matthew consistently increased his ability to recognize when help was needed and requested help in 100% of opportunities with minimal to no cueing.
Increase the use of verbal communication to express thoughts and responses when given verbal and physical prompts	Asking Matthew to talk about how he felt about something	Instead of "shutting down," Matthew was able to independently report feelings of anger, frustration, and joy by the end of the semester.
Develop and use strategies to request help during 70% of opportunities with minimal cueing	Directly teaching compensatory strategies when Matthew "shut down"	Matthew was initially unable to use compensatory strategies when he "shut down." At the end of the semester, he was able to use such strategies with minimal or no cueing in 100% of opportunities.

continued on next page

Functional Strategies and Goals

Table 6.1, continued Matthew's Treatment Protocol

Goal	Method	Results
Increase intelligibility during functional communication activities by slowing the rate of speech when asked to repeat a message during 70% of opportunities	Asking Matthew to repeat a message slower when his speech was unintelligible	Matthew was able to slow his rate of speech when asked and was occasionally able to self-correct his fast rate of speech.
Demonstrate appropriate nonverbal interaction, including eye contact and body language, during 70% of opportunities when given moderate verbal and physical cues	Giving Matthew direct verbal cues, such as "Look up," and physical cues, such as lifting his chin	The frequency of required cues decreased by the end of the semester. Matthew was able to engage in appropriate nonverbal interaction when given minimal to moderate verbal and physical cues in 100% of opportunities.
Decrease impulsivity by stopping and thinking before providing a response for 70% of opportunities when given moderate verbal and physical cues	Providing verbal cues, such as "stop" and "think better," as well as demonstrations of impulsivity in others	Initially, Matthew failed to consider the consequences of his actions. Over the semester, he was able to decrease the frequency of impulsive behaviors and began to verbally cue himself to "stop and think."
Respond appropriately when given two choices when unable to or unwilling to initiate a next step during 70% of opportunities	Providing a forced choice when unable to form or initiate a plan	Matthew required forced choice options at the beginning of the semester, but not during the last six weeks of the semester.
Successfully execute a plan to complete a task with 70% accuracy with moderate cues within the allotted time	Providing cueing techniques and changes in room layout to facilitate attentiveness	With increased attention due to the room layout, cues provided, and an increased ability to ask for help when needed, Matthew was able to successfully execute tasks in 100% of opportunities when given minimal to moderate physical and verbal cues.

The Source for Development of Executive Functions
Copyright © 2005 LinguiSystems, Inc.

Functional Strategies and Goals

▶ **Child with Executive Function Deficits Associated with Asperger's Syndrome**

Background Information
Ryan was a six-year-old boy diagnosed with autistic spectrum disorder characterized by Asperger's syndrome tendencies with concomitant executive function and pragmatic deficits. Treatment goals focused almost primarily on executive function skills:

- Increasing self-awareness and regulation
- Controlling impulsivity and interruptions
- Modifying social behavior to fit changing circumstances
- Engaging in reciprocal play that is in tune with other's emotions and needs
- Increasing eye contact
- Increasing the complexity of problem-solving skills
- Improving speech intelligibility via articulation and rate production

Table 6.2 Ryan's Treatment Protocol

Goal	Method	Results
Demonstrate appropriate requesting skills with 90% accuracy	Using environmental constraints, such as withholding toy parts until Ryan made an appropriate verbal request Reinforcing self-control of impulsivity	Ryan's ability to appropriately request items increased from 60% to 92% accuracy when given minimal verbal cueing.
Demonstrate interactive turn taking during play with 90% accuracy	Using Legos and puzzles that require turn taking	Initially, Ryan demonstrated turn-taking skills 50% of the time and required many verbal prompts. By the end of the semester, Ryan spontaneously demonstrated turn taking for 90% of opportunities.

continued on next page

Functional Strategies and Goals

Table 6.2, continued Ryan's Treatment Protocol

Goal	Method	Results
Identify other people's emotions with 80% accuracy	Identifying emotions based on facial expressions Making a "feelings scrapbook," using pictures of Ryan displaying a variety of emotions	Ryan increased his ability to identify emotions from 67% accuracy to 94% accuracy.
Identify other people's feelings when presented with a situation with 90% accuracy	Using pictures, Ryan's feelings scrapbook, and games	Although Ryan demonstrated difficulty identifying emotions in a situation he had not yet experienced, by the end of the semester, he was able to identify other people's feelings in a situation with 92% accuracy.
Use appropriate social greetings at the beginning and end of each session	Providing verbal prompts	When given minimal verbal prompts, Ryan was able to use social greetings. However, when cues were not provided, Ryan would not use social greetings and eye contact was minimal.
Identify problems with 80% accuracy	Using problem-solving pictures Role-playing to put Ryan in a problem situation	Ryan often confused a solution with a problem and would impulsively produce a solution when asked to state the problem. He also demonstrated difficulty seeing others' perspectives. By the end of the semester, Ryan identified problems with 75% accuracy.
Generate two solutions when given a problem with 80% accuracy	Using problem-solving pictures	Ryan increased his ability to generate solutions from 67% to 72%. Although Ryan was able to generate appropriate solutions, he was not able to execute them outside therapy due to poor impulse control.

continued on next page

The Source for Development of Executive Functions
Copyright © 2005 LinguiSystems, Inc.

Functional Strategies and Goals

Table 6.2, continued Ryan's Treatment Protocol

Goal	Method	Results
Produce "th" in isolation with 80% accuracy	Impulsivity, inattention, inflexibility, and disinterest in producing sounds limited the use of traditional articulation therapy methods. Ryan often argued with the therapist and expressed intense anger with these tasks (saying "I *hate* 'th'!", negotiating, refusing, crying, and yelling). Only negative consequences were successful in altering Ryan's behavior. Productions were impulsive and lacked attention to preplanning for motor placement of articulators.	Productions improved from 38% to 50% accuracy in isolation.
Produce "er" in isolation with 90% accuracy	Ryan's efforts were consistent with the behaviors described for productions of "th." Generally, productions could not be shaped or cued, as Ryan simply produced rapid-fire repetitions without stopping to listen, identify, evaluate, or preplan the next attempt. Ryan's only expression of self-regulation for articulation activities was found in his frequent statement of "I can't do 'er' and I hate it!"	Productions improved from 47% to 55% accuracy independently; tactile cues for increased labial tension increased productions to 89% accuracy in isolation.

Functional Strategies and Goals

▶ Child with Executive Function Deficits Associated with Caffey-Silverman Syndrome and ADHD

Background Information

Alex was an 11-year old boy who presented with multiple congenital abnormalities secondary to Caffey-Silverman syndrome. He demonstrated a moderate receptive/expressive language delay, with a severe language processing component and concomitant deficits in executive function skills.

Treatment goals for Alex were to continue work on concrete language processing skills and to improve functional expressive communication skills, as well as address the following executive function skills:

- Increase attention span
- Decrease impulsive thinking and behavior
- Increase self-awareness
- Develop compensatory strategies during functional tasks and social interaction

Table 6.3 Alex's Treatment Protocol

Goal	Method	Results
Name five similarities of two objects/pictures with 80% accuracy with no verbal cues	Teaching categories and verbal cueing	Alex's accuracy increased from identifying two similarities to naming five similarities with 80% accuracy when provided with moderate verbal cueing.
Name five differences of two objects/pictures with 80% accuracy	Teaching categories and exclusion	Initially, Alex was able to explain one difference between objects. By the end of the semester, he was able to name five differences with 80% accuracy when given moderate verbal cueing.
Name five objects in a category with 95% accuracy with no verbal cueing and when verbally presented with a category	Using verbal cues, such as redirecting for attention, phonemic cues, and first letter cues	Alex's ability increased from being able to name two items within a category to naming ten items with 100% accuracy and no verbal cueing.

continued on next page

Functional Strategies and Goals

Table 6.3, continued Alex's Treatment Protocol

Goal	Method	Results
Retell a story/passage using five details with 80% accuracy after listening to the story/passage presented by the clinician	Using frequent verbal cues to attend and listen	Initially, Alex was unable to retell any details from a two-sentence passage. By the end of the semester, Alex was able to identify five details from the passage when given maximal verbal cues to listen.
Increase speech intelligibility to 80% when given moderate cues to use a slow rate of speech and exaggerated articulation	Providing cues to use strategies to improve intelligibility in functional communication situations (due to weak breath support)	Intelligibility increased from 60% to 100% when provided with moderate cueing to use compensatory strategies.

▶ Child with Executive Function Deficits Associated with a Balanced Chromosomal Translocation, Expressive and Receptive Language Delays, and Mental Retardation

Background Information

Sarah was a 9-year, 5-month-old girl who had been in speech therapy since the age of 14 months. She was born with a balanced chromosomal translocation associated with developmental delays and mental retardation. She also demonstrated moderate-to-severe receptive and expressive language delays, as well as deficits in executive function skills. Sarah's current therapy goals included efforts to improve expressive communication for the following:

- Simple, short explanations and/or descriptions
- Auditory attention and verbal memory
- Language processing and organizational skills
- Functional communication exchanges
- Self-awareness and regulation
- Initiation
- Simple task completion
- Use of more appropriate vocal intensity

Functional Strategies and Goals

Executive function skills were characterized by deficits in initiation, flexibility, novel problem solving, sequencing, and planning. Treatment goals in executive function skills focused on the following:

- Communication repair strategies
- Verbal organization
- Self-awareness and self-cueing for vocal intensity
- Asking for help
- Seeking more information
- Requesting additional time

Table 6.4 Sarah's Treatment Protocol

Goal	Method	Results
Demonstrate accurate comprehension of the main idea and provide relevant details of a short story	Using picture cards to aid story retelling	At the beginning of the semester, Sarah was able to generate four relevant details, using picture cards and maximal cueing. At the end of the semester, she generated ten relevant details using the cards. When the cards were taken away, she explained ten relevant details and one irrelevant detail.
Demonstrate sufficient verbal organization and working memory skills to sequence picture cards related to a simple short story with 80% accuracy	Providing picture cards copied from a story and cues and prompts, as necessary, including repetitions of parts of the story and identification of incorrectly sequenced cards	Sarah's ability to recall the story increased enough so that she was able to begin work on sequencing and ordering the picture cards.
Make simple comparisons and associations between given objects and list items from a given category	Beginning intervention at the level of functions and progressing to attributes, using the language processing hierarchy	Sarah was able to identify functions with 100% accuracy. Her ability to name attributes increased from spontaneously naming an average of three attributes per object to spontaneously naming more than three attributes. She also demonstrated an increased ability to identify objects based on verbally presented attributes.

continued on next page

The Source for Development of Executive Functions
Copyright © 2005 LinguiSystems, Inc.

Functional Strategies and Goals

Table 6.4, continued Sarah's Treatment Protocol

Goal	Method	Results
Use and comprehend the need to use a communication repair strategy with 80% accuracy	Teaching the strategies of "Please, say that again" and "I need help."	Sarah was able to spontaneously use each repair strategy once during the semester.
Increase vocal productions when responding to questions and when involved in conversational exchange with 80% accuracy	Asking Sarah to repeat statements and to speak louder because she was not heard. Introducing an FM system at the end of the semester	Even at the end of the semester, Sarah continued to present vocalizations at the intensity level of a whisper. When the clinician's voice was amplified through the use of headphones, it was observed that Sarah's vocal intensity increased.

▶ General Impressions from Case Study Treatment Plans

- Traditional speech-language goals were targeted.
- Executive function skills were targeted at both specific and global levels.
- Methodologies included implementation of both environmental and compensatory techniques.
- Outcome progress was documented.

The treatment plans illustrate the importance of incorporating multiple types of speech-language goals. Very specific discrete language skills, such as listing items in a category or producing "th," were addressed in conjunction with executive function skills. The largest impact was achieved when the executive function skills allowed the child to functionally integrate the discrete speech-language gains.

Treatment to develop executive function skills doesn't have to be overwhelming. Many of the techniques are based on applying the common sense strategies that are used with young children. The difference is that by isolating and directly teaching executive function skills, an older child can learn to consciously focus on and improve in skills that are lacking. External rewards are not as necessary for motivation when addressing goals in the area of executive functions. The real-life payoff of feeling more comfortable and confident in educational and social environments brings a smile to most clients' faces.

Summary

Discussing specifics of executive function deficits with parents or teachers and jointly brainstorming suggestions can provide immediate relief in the home and/or school environment. In addition, the complexity of executive function skills becomes less intimidating and clearer through the use of visual diagrams. We have found it helpful to describe primary processing and secondary association areas of the brain via one of the analogies described earlier in this book (pages 7-10). Then we use a simple drawing of the brain (Diagram 7.1) to illustrate the movement of information from more posterior locales to the anterior-most part of the brain, where information is integrated and acted upon.

This chapter will summarize the concept of developing executive function skills in four phases. A sequence of diagrams are provided that you can use to help parents and teachers understand how executive functions integrate with other aspects of communication skills.

Phase 1: Processing of Information

The first idea to introduce is how the brain deals with information and how that relates to current education and intervention services. Diagram 7.1 can facilitate this discussion. The goal is to establish an understanding of treatments that have been initiated to address significant modality specific deficits.

Diagram 7.1 Lobes of the brain and learning modalities
Lateral View

Specific lobes of the brain carry primary responsibility for processing or attaching meaning to certain types of stimulation. The temporal lobe of the brain processes auditory language information; the occipital lobe processes visual information; the parietal lobe processes tactile information.

If the child is receiving speech-language therapy for more typically identified deficits, such as phonology, language, syntax, concepts, etc., objectives focus on developing better skills in the temporal lobe area. These foundation language abilities must be developed for a child to be successful in an academic environment. These language abilities are also fundamental to developing higher level executive function skills. The goal is always to resolve significant deficits in primary areas of communication before attempting to address executive function skills.

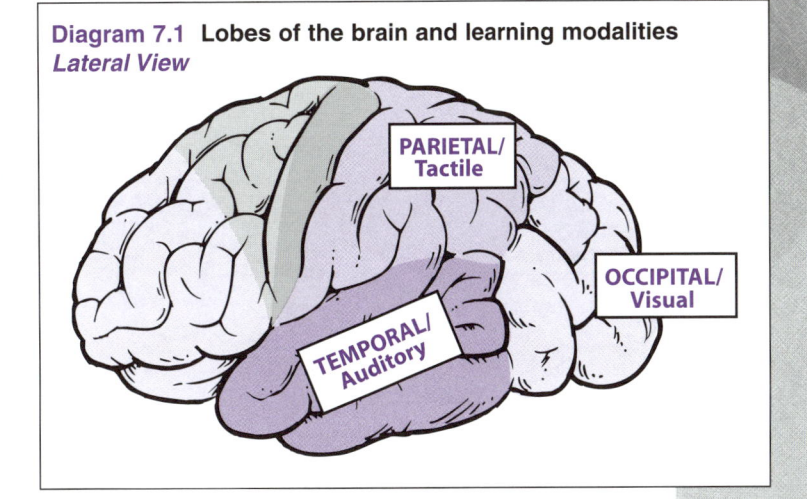

The Source for Development of Executive Functions

Summary

A child who is receiving occupational therapy services is receiving treatment to better deal with processing tactile sensation, which is focused in the parietal lobe. A student who is working on visual tracking or visual perception skills is receiving treatment to address better development of the occipital lobe. The basic development of these areas of the brain and the stimulation mediated within them is fundamental and prerequisite to higher level academic, interpersonal, and functional life skills.

Phase 2: Integration of Information

The next idea to introduce is the concept of integration within the specific modalities that is required to perform higher level academic and communication tasks. For example, reading requires that a student process visual symbols from the occipital lobe with stored language meaning in the temporal lobe to comprehend something presented on the pages of a book. Diagram 7.2 illustrates what the brain does with incoming stimulation.

Diagram 7.2 Integration of information across lobes of the brain
Lateral View

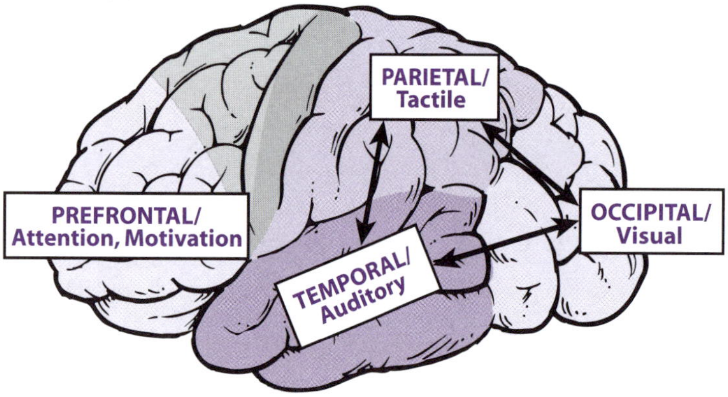

Most academic tasks require integration of information received. A child sitting in the classroom is constantly receiving multiple types of sensory stimulation. A teacher might be demonstrating something while talking. The student has to listen and watch to adequately understand what the teacher is presenting. If they are doing an experiment, the tactile input from the hands-on experience must be combined with watching the teacher's model and listening to directions being given.

In addition, some broad areas of brain involvement begin to have an impact in Phase 2. Attention to the task is important so that the child is able to accurately process information presented. The emotional motivation to want to attend and learn also becomes a factor. These skills are mediated in the prefrontal cortex. They interact with modality specific information (i.e., visual, auditory, tactile) in either a positive or a negative way. If a child doesn't care about a particular subject or chooses not to pay attention, then the content introduced will be compromised. In this case, the difficulty encountered isn't due to poor processing, but instead due to the negative impact of poor motivation and attention. It becomes more challenging for teachers and parents to discriminate the source of problems

Summary

when learning enters Phase 2, due to the interaction of multiple variables impacting performance. Teachers and parents will often comment that "I know she can do it" or "I know she understands that material; why does she perform so poorly in the classroom?" The impact of other variables can compromise adequate abilities in a negative manner at this level.

A student must develop certain competency in discrete skills for processing visual, tactile, and auditory information. The next layer of development requires the child to integrate information across modalities to achieve a higher level of complex understanding.

Phase 3: Integration of Information Across Modalities

In this phase, the frontal lobe mediates a child's response to the stimulation, processing, and integration that has been completed cognitively.

All the information processed and integrated in the parietal, temporal, and occipital lobes has to be organized and formulated into a concrete behavioral response. It is then sent to the frontal lobe where executive function skills reside. (See Diagram 7.3.) A response must be organized and planned, then motor programmed, and accurately executed. The response involves the motor strip to formulate a gesture/body response or a verbal response. The prefrontal variables of attention and motivation also influence the ability to functionally organize and monitor an appropriate response.

The neurological integration required is obviously more complex, with many more possible sites to encounter breakdown or difficulty. Situational cues that are often subtle must be processed and integrated with more concrete fundamental information. A child must adequately retain all these variables to generate options and determine the best solution. The multiple layers begin to present problems, which is why so many students experience difficulty at the level of developing executive function skills.

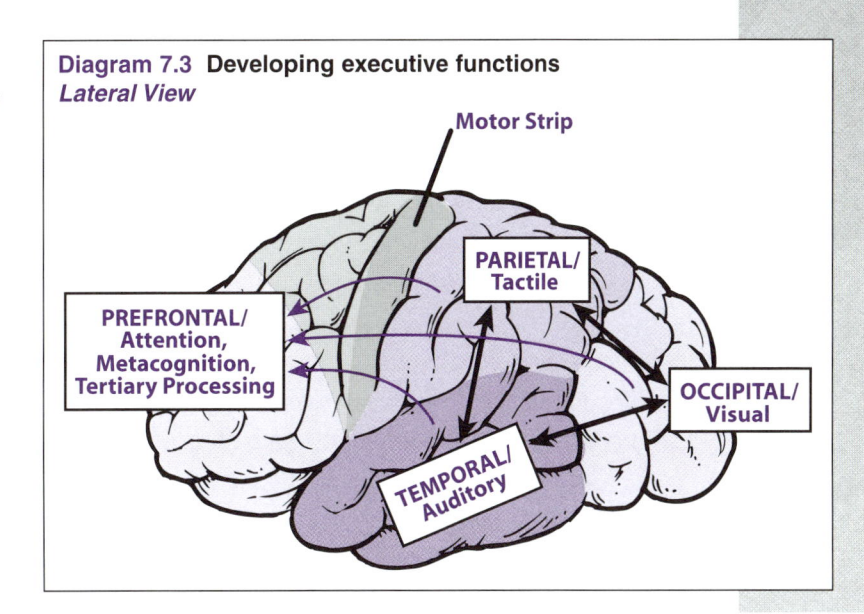

Diagram 7.3 Developing executive functions
Lateral View

- Motor Strip
- PARIETAL/Tactile
- PREFRONTAL/Attention, Metacognition, Tertiary Processing
- OCCIPITAL/Visual
- TEMPORAL/Auditory

Summary

Phase 4: Coordination of Multiple Variables

While the process is complex, Diagram 7.4 helps to illustrate the multiple variables that must be under coordinated control or that can be compromised when the cognitive complexity becomes overwhelming for the child.

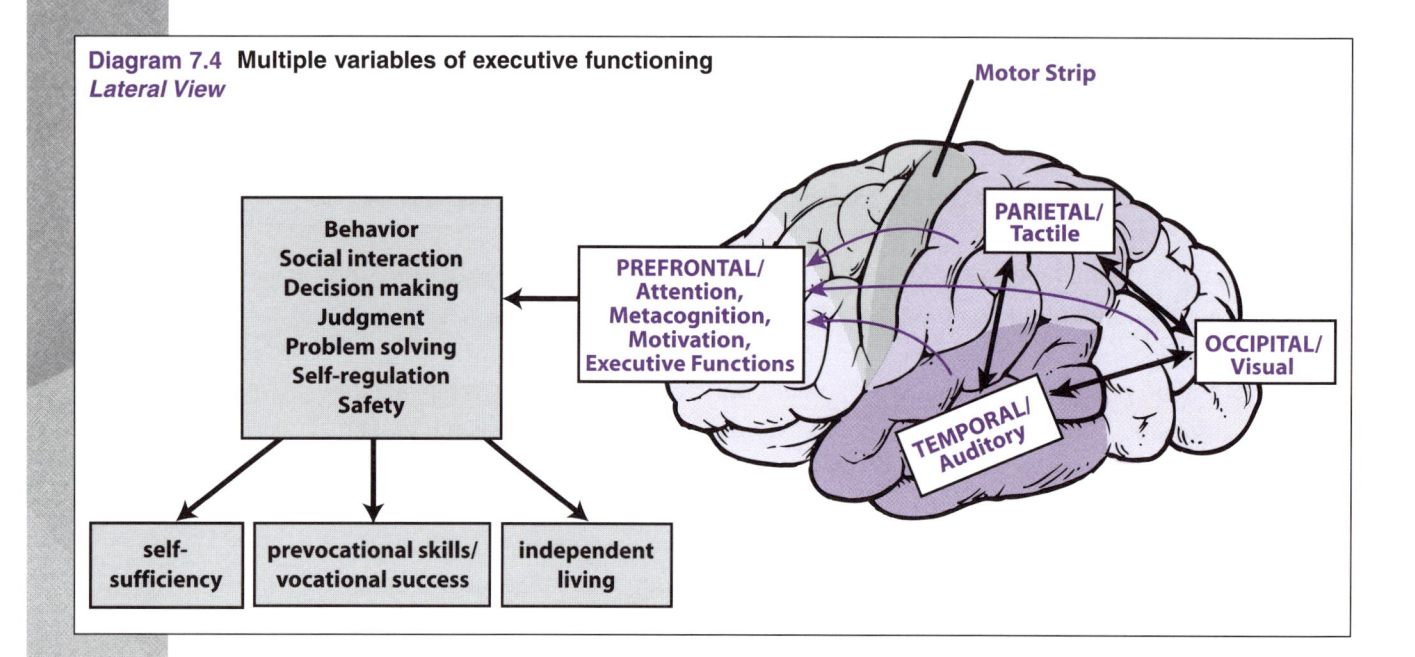

Diagram 7.4 Multiple variables of executive functioning
Lateral View

- Behavior
- Social interaction
- Decision making
- Judgment
- Problem solving
- Self-regulation
- Safety

PREFRONTAL/ Attention, Metacognition, Motivation, Executive Functions

Motor Strip
PARIETAL/ Tactile
OCCIPITAL/ Visual
TEMPORAL/ Auditory

- self-sufficiency
- prevocational skills/ vocational success
- independent living

This diagram allows parents and teachers to see how the development of executive function skills begins to impact the long-term prognosis for their child. If the child is struggling with phase 3 integration, a domino effect occurs into functional everyday living skills. The child who cannot modulate and regulate his emotional responses will be perceived as a behavior problem. The child who doesn't process environmental cues accurately will be defined as a risk taker with little regard for safety.

Society and school labels tend to focus on the symptomatic outcome of poor executive function deficits. However, simply punishing a child for displaying inappropriate behavior does nothing to address the reason that the problem is occurring.

Summary

> Consider the child with fetal alcohol syndrome (FAS) who evidences all the central nervous system impairments associated with that disorder. Being aware of the developmental neurological challenges that accompany FAS can prepare a caregiver or professional working with the child to know what to expect. They can also circumvent some of the problems if they begin addressing them early in intervention. Research is suggesting that some of the plateaus associated with FAS begin to disappear when treatment is initiated early to anticipate and resolve some of the symptomatic characteristics, particularly the behavior problems due to executive function deficits.

Concluding Remarks

The development of executive function skills was generally taken for granted in past decades. It either developed in response to natural environmental stimulation or the child experienced limitations and deficits throughout life. Sometimes an astute parent or teacher would recognize a child's innate capabilities that weren't being realized, and they would assume responsibility for directly teaching these subtle skills.

Advances in neurological understanding of the brain's development have led to more intense scrutiny and analysis of childhood deficits when they occur. Accountability has led to increased responsibility for professionals to address and remediate deficits. The area of executive functions is relatively new as a defined skill, but the expectations inherent within executive functions have always been present. For whatever reason, professionals are encountering more and more children who experience problems in developing executive function skills.

While development of executive function skills is an aspect of treatment that we should include in almost any language therapy plan, it should not be defined as the actual disorder. To label a child as having an "executive function disorder" implies that no other aspects of learning or language are involved; this area of development is the only one that the child failed to acquire. Unless the child previously demonstrated adequate and appropriate development of executive function skills, it is not a disorder unto itself; it is a result of other deficits or an acquired injury.

Summary

Problems in executive function skills are a natural outgrowth of other more specific deficits. The co-morbidity chapter illustrated this point by showing that deficits in development of executive function skills is fairly typical in many types of disorders. Children fail to acquire executive function skills due to other limitations in their developmental pattern. The diagrams included on pages 179-182 can help explain why executive function skills are usually compromised and need to be addressed in multiple stages of treatment. Expectations increase over time as the child grows older.

Speech-language pathologists (SLPs) become the primary professionals responsible for addressing development of executive function skills. Parents and teachers expect these skills to be present, but they don't know what to do when they aren't. Many SLPs have been addressing the aspect of executive function for years but called it something else. In adults who demonstrated these skills and lost them due to injury, executive function skills become a large component of treatment. When SLPs overlooked this area, they were somewhat frustrated with their treatment results. While specific speech-language goals were met, the functional impact was disappointing. The aspect missing in treatment was the generalization encompassed within executive functions.

As a profession, we can have a significant impact on an individual's life by elevating treatment goals to another level—executive function skills. We must realize that communication goals need to be relevant to the requirements of culture, society, and life in general. We can facilitate dramatic, life-altering accomplishments!

Resources for Formal and Informal Assessment

- *Behavior Rating Inventory of Executive Function.* Gioia, G.A., Isquith, P.K., Guy, S.C., & Kenworthy, L. Lutz, FL: Psychological Assessment Resources, Inc.

- *Behavior Rating Inventory of Executive Function—Preschool.* Gioia, G.A., Espy, K.A., & Isquith, P.K. Lutz, FL: Psychological Assessment Resources, Inc.

- *Behavior Rating Inventory of Executive Function—Self-report.* Guy, S.C., Isquith, P.K., & Gioia, G.A. Lutz, FL: Psychological Assessment Resources, Inc.

- *Behavioral Assessment of the Dysexecutive Syndrome in Children.* Emslie, H., Wilson, F.C., Burden, V., Nimmo-Smith, I., & Wilson, B.A. Suffolk, England: Thames Valley Test Company.

- *Children's Color Trails Test.* Llorente, A.M., Williams, J., Satz, P., & D'Elia, L.F. Lutz, FL: Psychological Assessment Resources.

- *Competing Sentences Test.* Carver, W. St. Louis, MO: Auditec of St. Louis.

- *Comprehensive Assessment of Spoken Language.* Carrow-Woolfolk, E. Circle Pines, MN: AGS Publishing.

- *Conners' Continuous Performance Test.* Conners, C.K. Toronto: Multi-health Systems.

- *Controlled Oral Word Association Test.* Benton, A.L., & Hamsher, K. Newark, NJ: Gordon and Breach Publishing Group.

- *d2 Test of Attention.* Brickenkamp, B., & Zillmer, E. Cambridge, MA: Hogrefe & Huber Publishers.

- *Dichotic Digits Test.* Carver, W. St. Louis, MO: Auditec of St. Louis.

- *Duration Pattern Sequence Test.* Pinheiro, M., & Musiek, F.E. St. Louis, MO: Auditec of St. Louis.

- *Expressive One-Word Picture Vocabulary Test.* Brownell, R. (Ed.) Novato, CA: Academic Therapy Publications.

- *Goldman-Fristoe Test of Articulaton 2.* Goldman, R., & Fristoe, M. Circle Pines, MN: AGS Publishing.

- *Halstead-Reitan Neuropsychological Test Battery.* Reitan, R.M., & Wolfson, D. Tucson, AZ: Neuropsychology Press.

- *Low Pass Filtered Speech Test.* Carver, W. St. Louis, MO: Auditec of St. Louis.

- *NEPSY: A developmental neuropsychological assessment.* Korkman, M., Kirk, U., & Kemp, S. San Antonio, TX: Psychological Corporation.

- *Peabody Picture Vocabulary Test: Third Edition.* Dunn, L.M., Dunn, L.M., Williams, K.T., & Wang, J. Circle Pines, MN: AGS Publishing.

Resources

- *Pitch Pattern Sequence (or Frequency Patterns) Test.* Pinheiro, M., & Ptacek, P.H. St. Louis, MO: Auditec of St. Louis.

- *Porteus Mazes.* Porteus, S.D. San Antonio, TX: The Psychological Corporation.

- *Rey Complex Figure Test and Recognition Trial.* Reitan, R.M., & Wolfson, D. South Tucson, AZ: Neuropsychology Press.

- *Ruff 2 & 7 Selective Attention Test.* Ruff, R.M. & Allen, C.C. Lutz, FL: Psychological Assessment Resources, Inc.

- *Ruff Figural Fluency Test.* Ruff, R.M. Lutz, FL: Psychological Assessment Resources, Inc.

- *Stroop Color and Word Test.* Golden, C.J. Lutz, FL: Psychological Assessment Resources.

- *Stroop Color and Word Test: Children's Version.* Golden, C. J., Freshwater, S. M., & Golden, Z. Lutz, FL: Psychological Assessment Resources.

- *Test of Everyday Attention for Children.* Manly, T., Robertson, I., Anderson, V., & Nimmo-Smith, I. San Antonio, TX: Harcourt Assessment, Inc.

- *Test of Problem Solving—Elementary* (restandardized as *Test of Problem Solving 3: Elementary*). Huisingh, R., Bowers, L., & LoGiudice, C. East Moline, IL: LinguiSystems, Inc.

- *Time Compressed Sentence Test.* Keith, R. St. Louis: Auditec of St. Louis.

- *Tower of London DX: 2nd Edition.* Culbertson, W.C., & Zillmer, E.A. North Tonawanda, NY: Multi-Health Systems, Inc.

- *Trail Making Test* (a component of the *Halstead-Reitan Neuropsychological Test Battery*). Reitan, R.M., & Wolfson, D. Tucson, AZ: Neuropsychology Press.

- *Wisconsin Card Sorting Test.* Heaton, R.K. Odessa, FL: Psychological Assessment Resources.

- *Woodcock-Johnson III.* Woodcock, R., McGrew, K., & Mather, N. Itasca, IL: Riverside Publishing.

- *Woodcock-Johnson PsychoEducational Battery—Revised.* Woodcock, R., & Johnson, B. Itasca, IL: Riverside Publishing.

References

American Psychiatric Association (2000). *Diagnostic and statistical manual of mental disorders (4th ed., text revision)*. Washington, D.C.: American Psychiatric Association.

Anderson, P. (2002). Assessment and development of executive function during childhood. *Child Neuropsychology, 8*(2), 71-82.

Anderson, V. (2001). Assessing executive functions in children: Biological, psychological, and developmental considerations. *Pediatric Rehabilitation, 4*(3), 119-136.

Anderson, V., Anderson, P., Northam, E., Jacobs, R., & Catroppa, C. (2001). Development of executive functions through late childhood and adolescence in an Australian sample. *Developmental Neuropsychology, 20*(1), 385-406.

Barco, P.P., Crosson, B., Bolesta, M.M., Werts, D., & Stout, R. (1991). Levels of awareness and compensation in cognitive rehabilitation. In J.S. Kreutzer & P. Wehman (Eds.), *Cognitive rehabilitation for persons with traumatic brain injury: A functional approach*. Baltimore: Paul Brookes Publishing Company.

Brocki, K.C., & Bohlin, G. (2004). Executive functions in children aged 6 to 13: A dimensional and developmental study. *Developmental Neuropsychology, 26*(2), 571-593.

Casanova, Manuel F., Buxhoeveden, Daniel P., Switala, Andrew E., Roy, E. (2002). Asperger's syndrome and cortical neuropathology. *Journal of Child Neurology, 17*(2), 142-145.

Chelune, G.J., & Baer, R.A. (1986). Developmental norms for the Wisconsin Card Sorting Test. *Journal of Clinical and Experimental Neuropsychology, 8,* 219-228.

Diamond, A., & Goldman-Rakic, P.S. (1989). Comparison of human infants and rhesus monkeys on Piaget's AB task: Evidence for dependence on dorsolateral prefrontal cortex. *Experimental Brain Research, 74,* 24-40.

Eliot, L. (1999). *What's going on in there? How the brain and mind develop in the first five years of life.* New York: Bantam Books.

Eslinger, P.J. (1996). Conceptualizing, describing, and measuring components of executive function: A summary. In G.R. Lyon & N.A. Krasnegor (Eds.). *Attention, Memory, and Executive Function.* Baltimore, MD: Paul H. Brookes Publishing Co., Inc.

Gedye, A. (1991). Tourette syndrome attributed to frontal lobe dysfunction: Numerous etiologies involved. *Journal of Clinical Psychology, 47,* 233-252.

Hughes, C. (2001). Executive dysfunction in autism: Its nature and implications for everyday problems. In J. Burack, T. Charman, N. Yirmiya, & P. Zelazo (Eds.), *The development of autism: Perspectives from theory and research.* Mahwah, NJ: Lawrence Erlbaum Associates.

Kane, M., & Engle, R. (2002). The role of prefrontal cortex in working-memory capacity, executive attention, and general fluid intelligence: An individual-differences perspective. *Psychonomic Bulletin & Review, 9*(4), 637-671.

Klenberg, L., Korkman, M., & Lahi-Nuuttila, P. (2001). Differential development of attention and executive functions in 3- to 12-year-old Finnish children. *Developmental Neuropsychology, 20*(1), 407-428.

Knight, J.A., & Kaplan, E. (Eds.) (2003). *Handbook of Rey-Osterrieth complex figure usage: Clinical and research applications.* Lutz, FL: Psychological Assessment Resources.

Lezak, M.D. (1983). *Neuropsychological assessment* (2nd ed.). New York: Oxford University Press.

References

Luria, A.R. (1973). *The working brain: An introduction to neuropsychology.* Harmondsworth, UK: Penguin Books Ltd.

Marlowe, W.B. (2000). An intervention for children with disorders of executive functions. *Developmental Neuropsychology, 18*(3), 445-454.

Mesulum, M.M. (1985). *Principles of behavioral neurology.* Philadelphia: F. A. Davis.

Musiek, F., & Pinheiro, M. (1987). Frequency patterns in cochlear, brainstem and cerebral lesions. *Audiology, 26,* 79-88.

Nauta, W.J.H. (1971). The problem of the frontal lobe: A reinterpretation. *Journal of Psychiatric Research, 8,* 167-187.

Osterrieth, P.A. (1944). The Complex Figure Copy Test. *Archives of Psychology, 30,* 206-353.

Passler, M., Isaac, W., & Hynd, G. (1985). Neuropsychological development of behavior attributed to frontal lobe functioning in children. *Developmental Neuropsychology, 1*(4), 349-370.

Pennington, B.F., & Ozonoff, S. (1996). Executive functions and developmental psychopathologies. *Journal of Child Psychology and Psychiatry Annual Research Review, 37,* 51-87.

Rebok, G.W., Smith, C.B., Pascualvaca, D.M., Mirsky, A.F., Anthony, B.J., & Kellam, S.G. (1997). Developmental changes in attentional performance in urban children from eight to thirteen years. *Child Neuropsychology, 3,* 28-46.

Reitan, R.M., & Wolfson, D. (1985). *The Halstead-Reitan Neuropsychological Test Battery.* Tucson, AZ: Neuropsychology Press.

Rey, A. (1941). Psychological examination of traumatic encephalopathy. *Archives of Psychology, 28,* 286-340.

Richard, G.J., & Russell, J.L. (2001). *The source for ADD/ADHD: Attention deficit disorder and attention deficit/hyperactivity disorder.* East Moline, IL: LinguiSystems, Inc.

Rosenn, D. & Vacca, D. (2001, May). Connections and disconnections: Implications of learning and living with Asperger's syndrome (presented at the *Learning and the Brain IV Conference*), Washington, DC and sponsored by Public Information Resources, Inc.

Stuss, D.T. (1992). Biological and psychological development of executive functions. *Brain and Cognition, 20,* 8-23.

Thatcher, R.W. (1991). Maturation of the human frontal lobes: Physiological evidence for staging. *Developmental Neuropsychology, 7*(3), 397-419.

Wadsworth, B.J. (1989). *Piaget's theory of cognitive and affective development.* White Plains, NY: Longman, Inc.

Welsh, M., Pennington, B., & Grossier, D. (1991). A normative-developmental study of executive function: A window on prefrontal function in children. *Developmental Neuropsychology, 7*(2), 131-149.

Wood, J. (2003). Social cognition and the prefrontal cortex. *Behavioral and Cognitive Neuroscience Reviews, 2*(2), 97-114.

Ylvisaker, M., & DeBonis, D. (2000). Executive function impairment in adolescence: TBI and ADHD. *Topics in Language Disorders, 20*(2), 29-57.

Zelazo, P.D., & Mueller, U. (2002). Executive functions in typical and atypical development. In U. Goswami (Ed.), *Handbook of Childhood Cognitive Development* (pp. 445-469). Oxford: Blackwell.